"*Life, In Spite of Me* is a remarkable story of life beyond despair and hope that triumphs over tragedy."

—LOUIE GIGLIO, pastor, Passion City Church/The Passion Movement

"Suicide is a liar and a thief. It promises peace to those who are escaping but delivers unimaginable pain and rejection to those left behind. Kristen Jane Anderson's riveting story unmasks the thief and gives hope a face."

—DR. DENNIS RAINEY, president, FamilyLife Ministries

"When I first met Kristen, I was overwhelmed with her smile, and then I saw her wheelchair. It was a defining moment for me. I had not heard her story or why she'd ended up at Moody. But it was her smile—and it is still her smile—that dismantles me. Kristen has something. It is something otherworldly. She had every reason to die, but now she has every reason to live. I hope you'll read her story, see her smile, and know why she lives."

—MICHAEL EASLEY, former president, Moody Bible Institute

"Kristen's story is a great example of what a big God and the resilient human spirit can accomplish. *Life, In Spite of Me* is a must-read for anyone who struggles with self-doubt or insecurity. I have no question God will use Kristen to transform many lives."

—TRENT DILFER, Super Bowl XXXV champion quarterback and TV sports analyst

"Kristen's endearing personality and piercing vulnerability drew me in from the first page to the last. If you are in a pit of despair, this book will give you the strength to hold on. By giving voice to her struggles, Kristen shows that you are not alone and there is a God who sees and will not waste any of your pain. This book is going to save lives."

—NICOL SPONBERG, singer, songwriter, and former member of the Dove award-winning trio Selah

"From the first time I met Kristen, I knew she was an amazing young lady. As a fellow double amputee, I understand the difficulties she faces every day. Kristen lives with relentless joy and contagious optimism. Her story will infuse you with hope and a passion for life."

—RON SANTO, Chicago Cubs nine-time All-Star third baseman and radio broadcaster

"Kristen is a trustworthy guide through the difficult issues of depression, facing one's own choices, self-forgiveness, and discovering authentic faith. Her recovery isn't a mountaintop experience others are incapable of having, but a real story of perseverance through fear, setbacks, and disappointments. She is an honest and credible teacher for all of us."

—DR. JOANN NISHIMOTO, clinical psychologist

"An incredible, heart-wrenching story about an incredible God who is always there, however dark it is, and how—standing in the shadows—he saved, healed, and restored his daughter to become a healing agent in a hurting world. A must read."

—JILL P. BRISCOE, author and speaker

Life,
In Spite of Me

Life, In Spite of Me

Extraordinary Hope After a Fatal Choice

Kristen Jane Anderson
with Tricia Goyer

MULTNOMAH
BOOKS

Life, In Spite of Me
Multnomah Books
12265 Oracle Boulevard, Suite 200
Colorado Springs, Colorado 80921

This book is not intended to replace the medical advice of a trained medical professional. Readers are advised to consult a physician or other qualified health-care professional regarding treatment of their medical problems. The author and publisher specifically disclaim liability, loss, or risk, personal or otherwise, which is incurred as a consequence, directly or indirectly, of the use or application of any of the contents of this book.

Details in some anecdotes and stories have been changed to protect the identities of the persons involved. Names and identifying characteristics of some people have been changed. For the sake of narrative flow, time lines have been condensed or modified.

ISBN 978-1-60142-363-4
ISBN 978-1-60142-253-8 (electronic)

Published in association with the literary agency of Janet Kobobel Grant, Books & Such, 52 Mission Circle, Suite 122, PMB 170, Santa Rosa, CA 95409. www.booksandsuch.biz

Published in the United States by WaterBrook Multnomah, an imprint of the Crown Publishing Group, a division of Random House Inc., New York.

The Library of Congress cataloged the hardcover edition as follows:
Anderson, Kristen Jane.
Life, in spite of me : extraordinary hope after a fatal choice / Kristen Jane Anderson, with Tricia Goyer.—1st ed.
p. cm.
ISBN 978-1-60142-252-1—ISBN 978-1-60142-253-8 (electronic) 1. Anderson, Kristen Jane. 2. Christian biography—United States. 3. Suicidal behavior—Patients—United States—Biography. 4. Amputees—United States—Biography. I. Goyer, Tricia. II. Title.
BR1725.A342A3 2010
248.8'628092—dc22
[B]

2009051643

Printed in the United States of America
2010—First International Trade Paperback Edition

10 9 8 7 6 5 4 3 2 1

To God. You are the reason that I live.
Thank you for everything you are. I will love you forever.
To anyone who has ever questioned the point to life
or wondered why you're alive,
and to those who want to help the hurting.
This book is for you.

Contents

Life

Dear reader,

This is my story. Sometimes it gets a little crazy...you'll see, but my guess is that in many ways my story and yours are not that different.

Between some of the chapters you will find personal notes from me to you. These include things I wish I had known, things I wish someone had told me back then. I hope you will find what I've shared encouraging.

I am praying for you.

Kristen

1

Life

Just Let Me Die

Numb. The cold Illinois wind chilled my body.

Numb. My mind, my heart.

At just past 6:00 p.m., the sky was black, and the icy January air hovered over the ground as a thick, misty fog. Snow clung to the dirt in patches, and my heart felt as dead as the wintry world around me. Silently, I trudged through the park and tugged my knit gloves tighter. I wanted only to be happy and for life to be a little easier, but everything seemed to be getting worse.

On one side of me, the park was dark and silent. Once full of life and laughter, my soul was the same. Play equipment, empty and laced with frost, sat motionless. In the other direction, lights from the town attempted to penetrate the fog. The idea of going home caused a heavy weight to sink in my stomach. I didn't want to face my parents.

Or my life.

Cold seeped through my jeans and coat as I sat down on the hard wooden seat of a nearby swing. Frozen chains creaked softly, and my thoughts took me back to all the times I'd played at this park during happy childhood days—too many to count. Now I was seventeen; those days were long past.

Why does life have to be so painful?

I turned in the swing, twisting the chains above my head tighter and tighter. Then I released. My body unwound in a slow turn. If only the invisible chains wrapped around my heart would free as easily.

A car drove by, and my body tensed. The park closed at dusk. Policemen patrolled the area, and I knew if they found me they'd send me home.

I don't want to go back... I just can't do it.

I'd never hung out in this park at night before. I didn't like being there, but I had no idea where else to go. I just needed time—time to figure out what to do next.

My gaze turned to the two sets of railroad tracks at the edge of the park. The first set of tracks was empty. A cluster of six cars sat on the second set. I knew the cops wouldn't be able to see me there.

Sluggishly, I made my way over to the line of railroad cars. My eyes zeroed in on the last car. I climbed up the side of it and sat, dangling my legs. I'm not sure how much time passed. Maybe an hour, maybe two. The danger of sitting on the train car put me on edge. After all the years living so near the railroad tracks, I'd never ventured this close.

I blew warm air into my hands, trying to thaw them, but it did little good.

What's wrong with me?

Everyone else seemed to be able to handle the burdens, the struggles of life, better than I could. All I wanted was to be happy. To have the perfect life I always thought I had when I was a kid. But my arms had grown tired from trying to hold my fantasy world together.

Lately, it seemed I couldn't do anything right. I wasn't there for my friends and family when they needed me. I was doing horribly in school, and I'd become a worry to my family. Now I was "grounded until further notice." I pushed the most recent argument with my parents out of my mind. And then there was the pain that ran even deeper than that. Memories too painful to think about. I pushed them back below the surface, as I had for months. In the past year I'd started smoking, drinking, and partying with my friends on the weekends, futilely trying to escape the pain.

I looked down at the railroad tracks and remembered a time I'd realized the power of a train. *A train would kill anyone in an instant. No one could survive that. If I ever wanted to take my life, if ever...that's the way I'd do it.*

The cold air around me brought me back to the moment. A deeper chill settled into my bones—and my thoughts grew darker; I knew I didn't want anyone to worry about me anymore. More than that, I wanted the pain to stop.

If I ever want my life to end...this would be my chance.

It's not going to get better. There's no reason I need to be here. There's nothing I'm supposed to do here. They'd be better off without me.

I tried to think of a reason to stay around, to live, but I could think of only one, my two nephews.

I'm not a very good example anymore. They're probably better off without me anyway, and I don't have any kids of my own. No younger brothers and sisters either. There's nothing important I'm supposed to do. My family, my friends… They'll get over me, right? I'm just causing pain and problems.

I looked around again at the cold, dark night.

This night is icky.

The world is disgusting.

My life sucks.

It could all be over soon, and then I won't hurt anymore.

I thought about school the next day. The homework I hadn't done.

I'm such a failure.

Do I want my life to end? If the train comes, should I end it?

Conflicting thoughts ping-ponged, faster, faster.

It's going to get better.

It isn't going to get better.

There's a reason I'm here.

There's no reason I'm here.

There's something I'm supposed to do here.

There's nothing I'm supposed to do here.

I was cold, and it was late. I wanted to leave, but I didn't know where to go.

Suddenly, a train whistle split the air. My heart pounded. I hadn't expected the train. Not yet. I still hadn't decided what to do.

I knew it would be a long time before the next train. *This is my chance.*

The thoughts came as fast as the train speeding toward me.

I'm so cold. This might be the only train for a while.

If I did it, the pain, the heartache, the numbness would be over.

I'm gonna do it. Soon it will all *be over.*

I stood between the parked train cars. I glanced across the dip between the tracks I was on and the ones the approaching train was speeding down.

I waited until the train got closer. I didn't want the engineer to see me. I didn't want him to stop the train. The large outline of the train's engine was barely visible beyond the bright headlight. It was almost here.

Heaven waited for me. I was sure of it. I was a good person.

Heaven has to be better than this life.

My heart pounded as I ran up the small bank. The train's headlight illuminated me. Its horn blared. I tried to push down the fear and shame, turned my face away from the train, and lay facedown.

I clenched my fists, crossed my arms under my head, and braced myself, closing my eyes tight. My head and body lay between the tracks, my legs hung over the rail. I could feel the cold metal against my thighs and the wood and rocks under my stomach. As the train closed in, the ground shook so much that my whole body vibrated. Then the train was upon me, over me.

Pain overwhelmed me. The train roared.

The momentum of the cars pulled at me, as if the train were trying to suck me into itself. The wind tugged harder, wrenching at my jacket and yanking my hair upward. My body rose, lifting slightly.

Then, even more powerful than the wind and the momentum of the train, another force pushed me to the ground. My head and chest hit first, then my hips and legs. Again I felt the power of the train, the shaking of the ground, the roar of it moving over me. The force of the weight pushing me down hurt more than anything else.

Fear coursed through me. I squeezed my eyes tighter.

It's going to be over now. The pain is going to end. I'll be in heaven soon.

As the whistle blew again, the vibration of my body stilled.

The sound stopped. The wind stopped. The train stopped.

Am I dead yet?

I opened my eyes and looked around. All I could see was train—beside and above me—dark, dirty, oily, but not moving.

Train cars stretched endlessly down the tracks in both directions. To my left, the closest train wheel was two feet away. To my right, an opening between the wheels revealed something next to the tracks. My jeans. And the bright white tennis shoes I got for Christmas.

Disbelief filled me. I was looking at my legs…lying about ten feet away.

This is a horrible nightmare. I need to wake up.

Suddenly, I had to get out from under the train. I felt claustrophobic; everything was closing in. The smell of hot metal and smoke was suffocating. I didn't know what was real, what wasn't. I couldn't think. I didn't know what to do.

I tried to move my legs to propel myself out. I couldn't. I lifted my right knee and tried to crawl out, but fell flat.

I have to get out of here…

I sucked in a breath, placed one arm in front of me, and then pulled my body toward it. I did it again with my other arm—army-crawling off the tracks. The pain was dull and deep.

I crawled off the tracks to the large black rocks that sloped beside them. I swung the bottom half of my body around, positioning my legs downward. I leaned back, half-sitting. Sharp rocks poked my back. Even in the cold night, I felt hot all over.

Behind me sat the ominous presence of the train.

I looked down, first to my left. I couldn't see anything except the ground. I looked to my right, and it appeared as if my right leg ended below the knee. Seeing only half my leg confused me.

I ran my hand below my knee. Nothing was there. My lower leg was gone. As I brought my hand back up to my face, something dark and shiny reflected off my knit glove.

Blood. The train must have cut off my legs. They are gone.

With that realization, the pain hit. It shot through me, sharp and deep, consuming all that was left of me—more pain than my mind could bear. Fear filled my heart.

I'm alive, and I don't have my legs.

Cries choked me, filling my throat and pouring from me.

"Mom. Mom! Mo-o-o-m!" I knew she couldn't hear me. No one could.

My body shook, and my cries became a scream. My hands trembled, my teeth clattered. Cold air hit my face. Heat consumed my body, especially my legs.

My cries became whimpers. "Help me," I mouthed.

I'd never felt so helpless.

I couldn't help myself even if I wanted to. And I did want to. I wanted to move. I wanted to run away from this nightmare. Heaviness settled over me, a mix of fear and disbelief.

My body felt heavy too, as if I were chained to the ground and couldn't stand up. My stomach sank deeper. My heart ached.

Then a new fear struck me. What if someone was looking for me? The engineer must have seen me, because he had stopped the train. I didn't want anyone to find me. I didn't want help. I just wanted to die.

I knew I must have been losing a lot of blood. Surely death would come soon. *God, let me die; just let me go to heaven.*

Frustrated tears overwhelmed me. Intense pain continued to course through me. The sobs came harder. I crossed my arms and laid my head on them, just as I had on the tracks. I turned onto my stomach, clenching my fists once again, and cried into my arms. Suddenly, a peaceful sensation flowed over me, as if a warm blanket had been wrapped around me. The comfortable presence was indescribable. I sensed that everything was going to be okay.

I could still feel the pain in my body, the aching of my heart, but it was in the background. The world around me was muted. *I must be dying. Maybe I'll be in heaven soon.*

A song filled my mind. There was no clear voice, yet there were words, sharp and clear, playing ten times louder than the music.

Amazing grace, how sweet the sound,
That saved a wretch like me.
I once was lost, but now am found.
Was blind, but now I see.

The song played over and over and over. I knew the end was near. It could only be music from heaven.

As the song ended, the peace remained. *This is it. This is the end.* I prayed I was a good enough person for heaven, hoping that I was. My body relaxed, and I felt lighter…lighter…

Then…a whisper of a touch on my face pulled me back to reality. Back to the moment. Back to the pain.

I opened my eyes, and they met with those of a rescue worker. His eyes widened, and his mouth dropped open. He stepped back slightly, as if unsure he believed what he saw.

Pain surged, and a war erupted within me. I was close to death, and I didn't want to come back.

Confusion filled my mind. *How can I still be alive?*

In an instant the man gathered himself, as if realizing what he needed to do. He looked toward the park and then slipped the radio off his belt. He spoke into it, giving his location and my status.

Anger coursed through me. I didn't want anyone to come. I didn't want anyone to save me.

"Over here!" he called.

Just let me die. I opened my mouth to speak, but the words didn't come.

The pain was unbearable. *It has to be over soon.*

A half-dozen rescuers hovered above me. Their intent, focused faces mirrored how serious my injuries were.

One man used scissors to cut away my coat. My favorite, yellow down coat. Small feathers fluttered everywhere, covering me.

Stop, leave me alone. Stop!

"What's your name?" A paramedic in a blue uniform approached.

"Kristen. Kristen Anderson."

"Are you alone?"

"Yes."

"What happened?" He leaned over me, looking into my eyes.

I swallowed hard, wincing from the pain. "The train… It ran over me."

The man turned away. "We need to stabilize her."

"An ambulance is on its way."

"Careful…watch her neck."

"She's lost a lot of blood."

"Call ahead and tell them it's a young, female patient. Legs severed…"

Watching everything, I was powerless. I felt like I was part of a television show, a movie, or a nightmare. It was surreal. This wasn't me. This was someone else. This wasn't happening.

I will wake up. But the pain told me it was real.

I felt vulnerable, helpless.

A radio crackled.

I couldn't see where the sound came from because of the fog.

My mind felt like that fog—cold and too thick to penetrate.

The voice on the radio cut in and out.

"On the count of three, let's get her onto this stretcher."

No! Don't help. Just leave me alone. Let me die.

"One, two, three…"

I braced to be moved, braced for the pain.

My body moved, and they carried me to the ambulance and loaded me inside.

Two people climbed into the ambulance with me.

I thought about my parents. I thought about the hospital bills. I didn't want my family to have to pay for the doctors to save me, especially when I didn't want to be saved.

My heart pounded as I looked around the inside of the ambulance. Someone took my hand. A woman's kind eyes peered down at me. "You'll be okay. Stay with us. Everything will be fine. Just hold on, sweetheart." Her words were gentle, concerned, motherly. A part of me clung to those words. Yet another part of me rejected them.

I looked away.

"You're going to be okay." Her voice was like a soothing balm, but I didn't want to be okay. I didn't want anyone working on me. Didn't want to go to the hospital.

Before I knew it, we were there. They quickly removed the stretcher from the ambulance and rolled it into the hospital.

A police officer hovered over me. "Why were you at the tracks?"

"I laid down in front of the train."

"Why?"

I hesitated. "My parents?"

Anger rose inside me. I knew it was so much more than that. It wasn't their fault. But how could I explain? I just wanted this man to leave me alone.

I glanced around as I was wheeled through the emergency-room doors and into a room on the left. It had large, yellow tiles on the walls. Medical equipment and machines filled the room. People hovered over me, touching me.

Go away. Leave me alone.

They moved me to another table. More needles. With their every effort I felt my space invaded, my body violated, my plans destroyed.

"Someone needs to call her parents." I couldn't see the woman who was speaking.

"What's your parents' phone number?"

I gave it to her, and she hurried away. I couldn't see her, but I could tell she was using a phone in the corner of the room. A minute later she was back.

"No one is answering at your parents' house. What's another number we can call?"

"You can call my sister, Stacey." I gave her that number too.

The paramedics had braced my neck, so I could only look straight up. Around me doctors and nurses worked. They stuck IV needles in me and hooked me up to various machines.

What is Stacey going to say? What is everyone going to think?

I pictured my sister picking up the phone, and my stomach turned. I imagined her being worried about me, scared.

The nurse's voice carried from across the room. "Yes, we have Kristen here. There's been a train accident. Please inform her parents. We suggest you get here as soon as possible. We're taking her into surgery."

A few minutes later, they wheeled me down the hallway toward the operating room. Everything smelled medical, disinfected, sterile. My mind raced back and forth.

Is this real or a horrible nightmare?

I watched the ceiling above me. Tiles and lights. Tiles and lights. They flashed by as we hurried on. Tiles and lights.

The doctor and medical personnel jogged at my side.

"Am I going to live?"

The doctor looked at me. "I don't know. You've lost a lot of blood."

If you're struggling with suicidal thoughts...

I know how you feel. Life is harder and more painful than you ever thought it could be. You're not sure if it's worth it, but I'm telling you there is so much to live for—more than you have ever experienced or imagined. Somehow, I hope my story will show that to you.

Please don't give up. You are not alone. There is a God who made you, and he's not as far away as you may think. He is always near. Wherever you go, whatever you do, he will be with you. He loves you, and he wants to comfort you, heal the hurt in your heart, and carry you through this life. Let him in.

God has an amazing plan for your life, even if you don't have a plan for yourself. He has hope for you, even if you don't have hope for yourself. He loves you immensely, even when you don't love yourself. And he sees beauty in you, even when all you see is a mess.

Suicide is never the answer. There is too much to live for. Keep fighting. Please don't give up. Reach out for help. You won't regret it. Your heart can be filled with hope, just like mine and so many others have been.

Love, Kristen

2

Life It Wasn't Supposed to Turn Out This Way

My eyes fluttered open, and I looked around. *Where am I?* My body felt heavy, as if a large weight had pushed me deep into the mattress. My mouth was dry, and I licked my lips.

What is my family doing here? My parents, brother, sister, and brother-in-law were standing around the room, arms crossed over their chests. Their faces were somber, and their eyes lowered. No one was talking; they were all looking down at the floor. *Something's wrong.* An ache settled in my chest. Not pain, but a deep knowing that I was the reason for their worry.

My mom looked up first, and our eyes met. She hurried to the side of my bed. All eyes lifted and turned in my direction.

"Honey, we're so glad you're okay." Her gaze was full of love and concern.

Why is she saying that? I heard her words, but I didn't understand what she was talking about. Then I remembered. I remembered crawling off the tracks, the crying, the pain. I remembered the rescuers.

"Mom, they cut my coat. They cut my clothes." I felt bad that my nice things were now ruined.

"Oh, sweetie, it's okay. We can get you new ones." My mom's voice was gentle. "We're just glad you're okay."

I heard her words but was too tired to respond. Her face faded to gray, and I felt myself slipping away.

It could have been hours or days that passed—I wasn't sure. I heard another voice, but it wasn't my mother's. "Kristen."

A man nudged me awake. My eyelids were heavy, but I struggled to open them and focus. I was lying on my right side, facing the window, my back to the man.

"Kristen, I'm your doctor. I need you to look at me. I need to tell you about your injuries."

I glanced over my shoulder to meet his gaze. I knew he didn't have anything good to tell me, and I didn't want to hear what he had to say. I looked away, instead focusing on the tall trees outside my window.

"Your left leg is severed well above the knee. And your right leg is severed below the knee. You may be able to walk again someday with the use of prosthetics."

I heard the words, but I didn't engage my heart or mind in what he was saying. I didn't want to talk about it. Or think about it. Sleepiness tugged at me, and I was all too willing to submit. I needed an escape from the truth.

My half-opened eyes fluttered shut, and sleep pulled me into its dark, consuming grasp.

When I woke again, it took a moment for my eyes to focus. White curtains covered a glass door. The curtains were partially open, and I could see part of the hall and a door to another hospital room. Flowers, balloons, and cards filled the table by my bed and the counter across the room.

Pink, red, blue balloons and varied bouquets brought brightness to the space. The scent of roses mellowed the hospital smell.

My mom stood by the table, straightening the cards. *Mom…*

My dad, sister, and brother sat in chairs. Everyone was quiet. My mind slowly cleared, as if layers of gauze were being unwound from my head, like the wrappings on a mummy.

My head was clearer, but I felt icky. My hair. My body. I wanted to get cleaned up. I felt awful and imagined I must look awful too.

I touched my face and felt dried mascara around my eyes, streaked from my crying. My skin felt crusty. Hair that clung to my face felt greasy. Dried blood flaked on my hand where they put in the IVs. More than anything, I wanted a shower. I wanted to be clean—to feel clean.

"Mom, can I call Kelley?"

Kelley had been a close friend since second grade. She was tall, thin, blond, and beautiful, and I felt more comfortable around her than anyone. We could always talk about everything. We'd often get ready together before we went out on the weekends. I knew she could help me. And I wanted her to be here with me.

My mom dialed Kelley's number on the hospital phone in my room, and then handed me the receiver. A moment later, my friend's voice came over the phone.

"Kelley?"

There was a moment of silence. "Yeah?"

"I'm at the hospital. Can you come do my hair and makeup?"

"Sure, I'll be right there." She hesitated. Her voice was shaky. "How are you doing?"

I looked down. My legs were still gone. I remembered seeing them lying by the tracks.

"I'm okay." My voice was quiet. I was fearful, and I didn't know how to tell her what had happened. It still didn't seem real.

"I'm okay," I said again, "but my legs are cut off." Tears streamed down my face.

"It's okay, honey," Kelley said. "You're going to be fine. You don't need your legs."

Her words offered a lot of hope, but after we said good-bye, questions plagued me.

How can I live my life without my legs? How could this have happened? Is this really real?

I wish someone would tell me it isn't.

The nurse's hands were warm on my arm. Her smile was warm too. She took my blood pressure, and then she took my temperature, using an ear thermometer. She checked the cords that were connected to my chest and adjusted the small clip on my finger that monitored my pulse. Machines circled my bed, and I knew they were keeping me alive.

"Are you comfortable, Kristen? Is your IV comfortable?" It sounded like she was speaking to me through a pillow.

"Um, yeah." Sleep, like quicksand, attempted to suck me back down. I forced my eyes to open wider. From the natural light softening the room, I figured it was either early morning or late afternoon. Beyond that I didn't know the time or the day. My mind fought to remember.

My arms felt as if they weighed a thousand pounds each. The pain was intense. I ached all over, but the pain in my legs was the worst. The deep, sharp, and stinging pains in my legs just wouldn't stop.

The nurse didn't explain what all the monitors and IV lines were for, and I didn't ask, as if asking would make this nightmare even more real than it already was. I didn't want to believe my legs were gone.

"I'm going to check the drains in your legs and change your bandages. I'll be as quick as possible and then you can rest."

I looked into the nurse's face, and she offered me a smile. Her voice sounded familiar, and I wondered if she'd been in my room often, taking care of me.

She moved the sheets off my body, and I glanced down. Blood-soaked bandages were wrapped around my legs. Tubes filled with blackish red blood stuck out from them.

I quickly looked away. My stomach turned, and I closed my eyes again. I felt tired, as if I hadn't slept for months, yet I also knew that all I'd been doing was sleeping.

My mom entered the room carrying flower arrangements in each hand.

"Are…are those for me?" My voice sounded gravelly, and the words came out slowly, as if someone had placed my voice on half speed.

"Yes, sweetie." She held up one of the arrangements for me to see. Roses, carnations, daisies, and greenery spilled from the vase. "Look, here are the flowers from Granny and Pappy. This basket is from the comptroller's office at the naval base." She placed it on a table alongside other gifts, and then held up a card so I could see it. There were many names on it, but I couldn't focus enough to read it. "Everyone from Dad's work signed it together, isn't that nice?" My pain throbbed in rhythm with her words.

I nodded, half-awake, attempting to understand what she was saying.

My eyelids grew heavy again. I tried to focus on the bouquet from my grandparents. *How sweet.*

I felt special, loved, cared for.

I managed to stay awake for a few minutes, but soon the medication overwhelmed me.

Closing my eyes, I slipped into the blackness.

Why is someone in my room in the middle of the night? My mind tried to focus.

I'd just awakened and was looking out the window at the snow, when I realized I wasn't alone. A girl sat near the window in a little chair, reading a book. I looked at her, wondering if I should know her. She had brown hair and a lot of dark eye makeup. I thought she was an illusion—a dark illusion.

I watched her for a while, and then it hit me: she was my sister. Stacey had come to be with me. "Stacey," my voice cracked, "your eye makeup looks really bad. You have way too much on."

"What?" The girl looked up from her book. Her eyebrows arched into two peaks. "Excuse me?"

"Your eye makeup looks really bad. You have way too much on," I repeated. I closed my eyes, and then opened them again, trying to refocus. Something didn't seem right. If she was my sister how come it didn't sound like her? look like her?

The girl shook her head in disbelief, and my mind worked to figure it out. Then I realized it wasn't my sister. I didn't know who she was.

Why is she in my room? What is she doing here? Where's Stacey? Where are my parents?

Sorry... I wanted to tell her. I opened my mouth, but the words didn't come out.

I closed my eyes and opened them one minute later—or at least that's how it seemed. A hint of sun peeked through the clouds, and the noise from the hall told me it was daytime. Things were always busier and noisier in the daytime.

My eyes closed and then fluttered open again. The sounds of someone moving around the room mixed with the noises of the nurses out in the hallway. My mom was straightening things. She had been in my room almost every time I woke up, talking to the nurses, making sure I was okay and that everything in my room was just so. The rest of my family was there too, as they had been during most of my waking moments.

Stacey was the quiet one in our family. It was easiest to read the worry on her face from the furrow of her brows and the tears that she tried to wipe away before I could see them.

My brother, Ryan, was outgoing and talkative. He walked in and waved. "Nice of you to decide to wake up from your nap." His smile was wide, and it settled me to see how normal he acted.

My dad looked at me, concern reflecting in his pale blue eyes as he reached over and squeezed my shoulder. I found the strength of his hand calm and reassuring, like a promise that everything would somehow be all right. I hoped that was true. Silently he rose, and then he bent down to kiss my forehead before turning to my mom. "Do you need something from the cafeteria?" They worked together in a natural way, both taking care of each other and watching over me.

"No, I'm fine."

"I'll walk with you." Ryan glanced at Stacey and stood. "Would you like anything?" He seemed taller than I remembered him being, and older, more mature.

"I'm fine," Stacey commented. She reached over and picked up a magazine from a side table and flipped through it, but I knew she wasn't reading.

Footsteps echoed on the hard tile floor as my dad and Ryan left for the cafeteria. Light played across my face, spilling in through the open drapes, and I looked toward the little chair near the window. I remembered the events of the night before, wondering if the girl had been in my room more than just last night. It didn't make sense. Why would she be there? I had a strange feeling she'd been there watching me, near me, more than once.

My doctor entered, walking to the side of my bed. His presence stilled my mother's movements. He was tall with brown hair. A white coat hung from his broad shoulders. He flipped through my chart, then pulled a pen from his pocket to jot something down.

"How are you today, Kristen?"

I didn't answer. Instead, I asked a question of my own.

"There was a girl in my room last night. Why was she here?"

He furrowed his eyebrows and then raised them, surprised. My mom and sister looked at each other and froze, waiting to see what he'd say.

"We have you on suicide watch. We need to keep you safe." He stated it as if it were obvious.

My heart sank. His words were almost like a slap to the face. I felt sick inside. It didn't seem right that no one had talked to me about this. *Does he really think I'd try to kill myself? Who does he think I am? Why would he say that about me?*

But with the hurt came confusion. *He wouldn't say that unless he thought it was true. Is that what he thinks happened? Is that what everyone thinks?*

"I don't want anyone in my room," I said flatly. The idea of someone I didn't know being in my room, watching me sleep, creeped me out.

"You don't think you need to be watched?" The doctor's face studied mine.

"No. I don't want anyone here. I don't need that." Yet even as I said the words, questions filled my mind. *Do I need someone to watch me?*

I could hardly stay awake, let alone think of a way to hurt myself. I replayed the events that got me there, but there were only scattered images. I remembered going to the park, but I had no memory of how I'd gotten *onto* the train tracks. The only other thing I remembered was seeing my legs several feet away from my body. *Did I try to commit suicide? Is that what really happened?*

Fear tensed my neck, and tightness spread over my shoulders and down my arms.

Why would I do that? Is that what my parents think too—what everyone thinks?

What if it were true? What if I really had attempted suicide? Shame caused a tightness in my chest and coldness to spread through me.

The doctor finished his examination and turned to my mom and my sister. "She's getting better. I'm going to change her meds a little, but it looks as if she's healing. She's not out of the woods completely, but it's a good start."

My family seemed pleased by this comment, but I wasn't. I didn't want to upset my parents, but the truth was, I didn't want to get better.

When the nurse entered, the doctor updated her on my progress. I could tell from his tone that things were still serious—that there was still no guarantee I would live.

Maybe things are too bad for them to save me. Maybe I'll just slip away. It still seemed better, easier.

No one showed up that night to sit by my bed, and I was glad. I had no plans to try to kill myself, but that didn't mean I wanted to live either. Especially now that I didn't have any legs.

When I woke up, I noticed that the balloons and flowers were gone. My eyes darted around the room, thinking that someone had just moved them. But there were no bright colors. No sweet smells. The cards with the notes my mom had read me from my friends, family, and people at church were all gone.

An ache filled my chest, and I tightened my hands into fists. Tears rimmed my eyes, and I wished I could turn over and hide my face in my pillow.

Why are they doing this? Are they trying to punish me?

I no longer felt special, loved, or cared for. It felt like someone was trying to hurt me.

My mom noticed me stirring. She moved to the side of my bed and took my hand, squeezing it, clinging to it an extra few seconds before letting go. The look in her eyes spoke what she'd said nearly every time I was awake. *I love you. I'm so glad you're here.*

"Mom, where are the flowers and the balloons? Where are my things?"

My mom had looked the same for as long as I could remember, with short brown hair and dark eyes. Everyone said I looked like her, and throughout my growing-up years, my friends told me they wished they had a mom like mine. She smiled often and spoke in soft tones. For most of my life, I hadn't seen her angry—or at least angry at me.

But now... Was she in on this punishment?

Mom's eyes were gentle. "We had to take them away, honey. Don't worry. Your cards and stuffed animals are all at home. I'm saving them for you."

"Why did you take them?" My mouth curled down. I knew they were just things, but all the gifts made me feel a little better. They were evidence of how much people cared. "I want them back. Can you go get them?"

"I'm sorry, Kristen." My mom rubbed her hand against her forehead, and then she reached for my hand, holding it, squeezing it. "The doctor said it was too stimulating. You need rest, sweetheart. You just need to think about getting better."

I felt my jaw tighten, but I didn't say a word.

Don't they know those are my things? How could they tell my mom to take them away? How could they be so cruel? Maybe they're doing this because of what I've done. They don't want me to be happy.

The balloons and flowers had been glimmers of comfort and hope. *What am I going to look at when everyone leaves at night?* Nothing. Only bare walls.

Sadness and confusion slid into a familiar numbness. Spikes of pain poked my heart for only an instant, and then I pushed everything deeper until it no longer hurt.

This isn't how my life is supposed to be. This isn't how my life was supposed to turn out.

I thought about everything that had led to this point. I'd had a wonderful childhood, a great family, and a good life, but like shadowed strokes over a Monet painting, disillusionment had gradually darkened the bright colors of my picture-perfect life. My innocence grew murky, as one pain after another swished away my naiveté. Not one dark brush stroke, but many, had brought me to this place.

As I lay there, my mind took me back to the beginning.

Life

3

Carefree No More

I placed my small hand in my sister's and focused on the peach-colored fabric of the maid-of-honor's dress as she walked down the aisle. Music drifted back from the piano near the front of the church that I'd attended as long as I could remember. I felt a hand on my shoulder and knew it was my time to walk. I looked up at Stacey, and her face brightened in a smile. She squeezed my hand and then released it. "Your turn, Kristen."

I glanced down at the rose petals and the pretty white basket I held in my hand, then looked up with pride. With each step I took, the puffy skirt on my princess dress swished and peach-colored petals fell from my hand to the floor. Everyone smiled as I passed. I was delighted to do my part to make my sister's wedding perfect.

I felt like I was flying as my white ballet shoes carried me over the orange carpet. The groom, Ken, was at the end of the aisle. He smiled at me and then turned his gaze to my sister who followed. Joy filled his face.

I was born the same year Stacey started dating Ken. She was fourteen and my brother Ryan was seven. For as long as I could remember, Ken had always been a part of my life. He'd play with me, and I'd climb all over him. It seemed only right he would officially be part of our family now.

Later, as my family gathered for photos, I smiled big, glad to be a part of it all. Proud this was *my* family.

In the receiving line everyone hugged my sister, and when they got to me, they shook my hand.

"You must be so happy, so proud," they would say. And I was. My sister was the most beautiful bride ever.

Standing outside the church, my mother handed me a flower with rice kernels nestled inside its silk leaves. As we waited for Stacey and Ken to exit, my throat felt tight and tears filled my eyes.

My mother knelt down in front of me and took my face in her hands. "Kristen, why are you crying? Is everything okay?"

"I don't know." My voice quivered. "I'm not sad. I'm happy." And that was the truth. Why was I crying? The emotions came when I didn't expect them. They were hard to understand. I was happy. Happy for my sister. Happy about everything.

A soft smile graced my mother's lips. "It's okay, Kristen. You can have happy tears too."

I swallowed hard and nodded. I'd never had happy tears before. Was that possible? I was used to crying when I was hurt or sad, but this was different.

And then, as my sister and Ken emerged from the church, I threw the rice out of my flower. It joined the rice from the others, sprinkling around their heads as they ran by.

"Come on, Kristen," my sister called from the limo. "You can ride with us to the reception."

The entire day I felt like a little princess enjoying a ball with my whole family. I laughed and sang and twirled and danced with my mom, my dad, and everyone else. My big brother even picked me up and danced with me a few times. Eventually my legs grew tired, and by the end of the night, I was exhausted. We left at midnight, and I fell asleep on the drive home.

When we got there, my dad carried me from the car to our front door, up the long, tall flight of stairs, and into my bedroom. I snuggled into his shoulder, feeling loved, cared for, and incredibly special.

My dad gently laid me on my bed, and I hoped that I didn't have to take off my beautiful white dress. I was seven. Life was perfect. I was a princess... or at least I felt like one.

I had an all-American, carefree childhood. I had everything I needed, almost everything I wanted, and no reason to think it wouldn't always be that way.

I loved my older sister and brother. My parents loved each other, and they loved me. We attended a small, traditional church together regularly. There I learned a lot about what was right and wrong. I learned that I wanted to be a good person—or at least do the best I could.

My mom worked for a health-care company, and my father was a budget analyst under the admiral in the comptroller's office at the Naval Station Great Lakes. I was proud of him. He looked so professional, so important, with his suit and briefcase. Serious and strong, he was also kind and affectionate. When I was little I'd wrestle with him at bedtime, and then we'd race to my room. Because I usually beat him, he gave me the nickname Speedy Two Shoes. My mom would meet us in my bedroom and together we'd say the Lord's Prayer. Sometimes I knelt as we prayed. Sometimes I'd lie in bed. My parents would stand or kneel beside me, and then we'd always hug and kiss goodnight.

"Sweet dreams, sweetheart. I love you." My mother's soothing voice would be the last one I'd hear as I drifted off to sleep.

It seemed like any other school night, any other family dinner, until I sat down and noticed my parents looking at each other in a way I wasn't used to. Their eyes seemed sad, and their lips didn't curl up in their typical smiles. My stomach tightened, but I pretended I didn't notice.

I was only in the fifth grade, but I knew something wasn't right. Things at home had been different lately. My dad seemed tired all the time and kept to himself. Sometimes my mom seemed lost in her own thoughts.

I placed my napkin on my lap and bowed my head for grace. As usual, together we prayed, "Come, Lord Jesus, be our guest, and let these gifts to us be blessed. Amen." Afterward, my dad cleared his throat. "Kids, there's something I need to tell you. I went to the doctor yesterday, and he found out why I haven't been feeling well."

I swallowed the food I'd been chewing and then set my fork on my plate. Fear filled my chest, taking over the space that my lungs needed to expand, making it hard to breathe. Neither of my parents had experienced health problems before. *What does that mean? Will he have to go into the hospital?*

I looked to my brother who was seventeen. His face was fixed on my dad's. I could tell my brother was worried too.

"I have something called hypothyroidism. It leaves me tired all the time."

I let that word repeat itself in my mind. *Hypothyroidism.*

I didn't know what hypothyroidism meant, except that it sounded bad. I continued eating, trying to pretend that the news wasn't bad and that everything would be all right.

"I'm also struggling with depression."

Ryan wiped his mouth with his napkin. "I don't think you're depressed."

"Yeah, I don't think you're depressed either," I piped up. "You're not sad all the time…"

"That's not really what it means, honey." My mom patted my hand.

It wasn't until later that I learned that my dad wasn't the only one in his family who had struggled with depression. We were on our way to church one day when I was fifteen; my parents had been talking about something else, and somehow the topic turned to depression and my dad's family history.

"You have an uncle who committed suicide, right?" my mom asked.

I sat quietly in the backseat, hoping they would keep talking. Hoping they didn't remember I was there and delay their talk for a more "private" time. I'd never heard of anything like this in my family before.

"I heard it was because his marriage was ending." My dad's voice was tight. The memory seemed to bother him.

"Your mom struggled with depression too." My mom glanced at him as he drove. We continued our trek to church, but I knew the conversation wasn't going to continue.

Though my dad's depression had become a part of our home life, its presence was mostly unspoken. By the time I was in high school, his depression was like a large dark object that everyone tiptoed around but did not discuss. I was never sure whether depression was something genetic in my dad's family or just something he struggled with, but I did know one thing: it was unpredictable. It went up and down. Some days he seemed fine. Other times I'd find him sleeping when I got home from school. I learned then that not speaking about it was better—or at least easier.

How could something unseen and unspoken have such an impact?

As I watched the houses, the roads, the familiar stores going by out the window, I thought about asking them more. *How did my dad's uncle kill himself? Was Grandma depressed in the same way my dad was? What does that mean for me?*

I walked into the homeless shelter with small steps, scooting closer to my mom.

The director smiled as she said, "Follow me, Kristen, and I'll show you where we'll be serving up meals." Inside it was quiet, but as I entered I spotted the line that was already forming outside. I sucked in a breath and for the first time second-guessed why I'd chosen this for my seventh-grade school project.

During the last year, social ills such as homelessness had filtered through the protective layers of my existence. I was beginning to understand that the world wasn't as happy or safe as I had grown up thinking it was.

"Here's an apron, Kristen." I put it on and got in line with the other volunteers—all adults—and placed rolls on the plates of those who went through the line—men, women, children. *I never expected kids…*

After dinner I helped set up the beds, which were actually just pads on the floor.

I can't imagine living like this.

I laid out the small pads, put a sheet on each, and then added a pillow. Others did the same. Bed after bed after bed.

How can anyone let their kids live like this? I thought of my bedroom back home with the white furniture set and pink flower comforter. Later, when I went home and slept in my nice room, the faces of the people at the shelter wouldn't leave my mind.

"Mom, can we collect food, you know, to take to the shelter?" I asked the next morning at breakfast. "I can ask all the teachers at school if it would be okay for me to set up boxes in their classrooms. Kids can bring food, and we can pick it up every Friday after school and take it to the shelter with us."

"That's a wonderful idea, sweetheart. I'll ask if I can put boxes at work and collect stuff there too."

Soon we did just that. I put boxes in the classrooms, collected food and toiletries, and took it all to the shelter. My mom got more stuff from work. At the shelter I served food and set up beds.

While working there made me grateful for what I had, I soon grew concerned.

"Mom, do you think that could ever happen to us?" I asked her one day. "Could we lose our house and everything and end up sleeping there too?"

"I don't think so, Kristen. We don't need to worry. That won't happen to us."

She said the words, but I wasn't convinced. *I bet these people never thought they'd end up here. They never planned for their lives to turn out like this.*

I also became discouraged. No matter how long or hard I worked, it didn't seem to make a dent in the need. There were too many people to help.

It's not right. I'm doing the best I can, but it doesn't seem to matter.

My heart hurt.

My work at the shelter wasn't the only thing that discouraged me. The more I learned in school, watched on television, or read in the paper, the more I discovered the world was filled with pain and suffering. Millions of people across the globe went to bed hungry every night. There was homelessness and sexual abuse. I was disillusioned by it all. An introspective thinker, I couldn't believe or understand how there could be so much pain, suffering, death, and disease in the world. It just wasn't fair, and it wasn't right.

It hurt to care.

I don't have to do this anymore, I told myself one night as I made beds.

I finished that night and didn't go back. I hurried to my mom's car, hoping to leave the dark cloud behind.

Don't think about it, Kristen. There's not really much you can do to help. You're only a kid. You did your best.

Instead, I tried simply to enjoy life, spend time with friends, and have fun being a kid. When my sister announced she was going to have a baby, I looked forward to being an aunt.

Focus on the good... Older and wiser people can worry about the problems of the world.

Unlike Cinderella, I had no fairy godmother who could make everything beautiful and perfect with one zing of a magic wand. But as long as I could push the problems out of my mind, keep them from distracting me, I was fine.

Life

4

What's Wrong with This World?

"Kristen, we just got a call from the nursing home. They said that Grandma Anderson doesn't have much longer. We're leaving right now to say our good-byes."

Our good-byes? I put my notebook down and followed my mom out of my room toward the front door. As we crossed the dining room, a picture of me and my grandma, taken when I was in second grade, caught my eye. I paused. It was hard to believe the photo had been taken nine years earlier. In the photo my grandma was sitting in a rocking chair in our living room, and I was on her lap. My hair was wet because I'd just gotten out of the shower. We were both smiling.

Not long after that photo was taken, she had a stroke, and she was moved into a nursing home near us. Because she was unable to walk or communicate for the past eight years, I never really knew her. Often we'd go to visit her as she sat in her wheelchair, and for holidays we'd bring her home to spend more time with us. Now it was hard to imagine that wouldn't happen anymore.

Ten minutes later we entered her room. It was strangely quiet. My grandma looked as if she was asleep. The only thing different from the other times I'd visited recently was that she was breathing harder than normal.

I stopped about four feet from the bed and froze, not knowing what to say or do. *Do I talk to her? touch her?* I was uncomfortable, so I did neither. Instead, I just stood there and watched the rise and fall of her chest. No one talked. We just watched her, reflecting on years past.

Thirty minutes after we arrived, she breathed out and didn't breathe back in again. My heart dropped; I looked around at everyone, unsure what to think.

Is she dead? In the movies there was always a beeping machine and a flat line on a screen. Here there was only silence.

My dad leaned over the bed. "Good-bye." His hands shook as he held his mother's hand. My mom did the same.

I still didn't know what to think. I silently said good-bye and then followed my mom into the hallway.

We got into the car and headed for home. My dad was silent. My mom wiped tears from her eyes.

"Is she, uh, dead?"

My mom turned and looked at me with a furrowed brow, as if she was unsure she'd heard me correctly.

"Yes, Kristen, I know it's hard to believe, but she's really gone."

My eyes filled with tears, and a deep remorse settled over me. *I should have visited more and spent time with her. Now I'll never have that chance.*

The funeral came and went, and over the next weeks and months it was a sad time around our home. Everyone was quieter, lost in their thoughts. We didn't talk about how we were feeling. *Is this pain, are these regrets normal?*

Was there something I could have done? Something to at least improve the quality of her life? Guilt overshadowed the sadness. Maybe if I had visited and helped her do more physical therapy, she would have done better. Maybe she could have walked and talked again. *Why didn't I go more? Why didn't I help?* Maybe she wouldn't have died if I'd only spent more time with her.

My guilt didn't ease as the days passed. I didn't know how to deal with a death in the family. Everyone else seemed to be handling it fine. Everyone but me.

"What's going on?" I'd just walked into the commons where the other high school juniors and seniors ate lunch and hung out in the morning. I wondered why my friends had circled up.

"It's Brandon. He killed himself last night. He hung himself from a tree at the cemetery. Kristen, he's dead."

I was shocked.

Brandon hung himself?

This can't be happening…

His face, his smile, filled my mind.

That isn't possible. Why would he kill himself? Things weren't that bad, were they?

This news was a punch in the gut, especially on top of the other deaths, illnesses, and problems in my life over the past year. People were dying all around me. My friend Justin's older brother, Brian, died in a motorcycle accident. And then another guy from school died in another motorcycle accident. Next, I found out that a girl named Tanya was in the hospital, dying of a brain tumor. I didn't know any of them very well, but they were all a part of my life in one way or another. Tanya and I had done some school projects together, and she was one of the happiest people I'd ever known. Before her, I hadn't known anyone my age who had cancer and was close to death. It was sad, scary. I didn't understand why all of them had to die. Especially at our age.

Why is all this happening? What's wrong with this world?

I knew there wasn't anything I could have done to save the people who'd died in the accidents...or even my grandma. But I was convinced I could have done something to help Brandon. We'd been friends for years. At the beginning of high school, he and I talked a lot. He liked my friend Cassie, and he would often call for advice about how to win her heart. We would talk about her, school, other friends, whatever, but I hadn't seen him around or talked to him as much lately. Some people said he was drinking heavily and had gotten into drugs. He'd been kicked off the football team, and his parents had just separated. I wished I'd known and had reached out to him or asked him how he was doing.

I should have been there for him.

Guilt became a constant companion. All of my friends felt the same, and we missed Brandon a lot. A week after his death, we found a way to be close to him, a way to show him how much we cared. We went to the tree where he had hung himself. The last place he'd been alive. The mood was somber as we entered through the cemetery's metal gate. "There it is." Someone pointed to the tall tree on the hill. Images flashed through my mind. My legs wanted to stop, but I continued on, walking alongside my friends.

Fear and sadness overwhelmed me, but I knew I needed to do this for Brandon. We sat around the tree and cried. Around us, in all directions, were headstones of others who had died. They'd lived their lives, and all it came to was a name on the headstone. I didn't want that for Brandon. He deserved better. What was he thinking as he tied the knots, securing the rope, securing his fate?

He can't be gone yet. This isn't how a good life should end.

Life

5

Small and Powerless

Three months after Brandon's death, life had returned to normal in many ways. I still felt a tightness in my chest when I thought of everything that had happened, but I dealt with the pain as best I could. Some days were easier than others, and today was one of the better days. I smiled as I climbed out of Kelley's car. The evening summer air was warm, and we took long strides as we headed to a party.

I took a deep breath and excitement built as we approached the door of Eric's house. He had called earlier that day inviting me and some friends over. I had no doubt there'd be alcohol at the party since Eric and his friends were of legal age to buy it. I'd tried a few drinks the year before, but after

Brandon's death I started drinking more. I used to tell myself that drinking helped numb the pain in my mouth when the orthodontist tightened my braces, but the truth was that the numbing effect helped me think less about *all* the pain in my life—or so I thought.

For so long I'd been such a good kid, a good daughter. Not anymore. There were a few times that my parents found out I had been drinking, and I didn't want that to happen again. I didn't want to get into trouble or have to explain. My mom had also discovered cigarettes in my jeans pocket when she did the laundry. I lied and told her they belonged to someone else, but I could tell from her eyes that she didn't believe me. I didn't like that look. I hated disappointing my parents.

The door opened. "Hey, come on in." One of Eric's friends smiled and stepped aside.

Almost before I could find a place to sit, someone put a beer in my hand. I found a spot on the sofa. Eric's eyes met mine from across the room, and I felt my heartbeat quicken. He was nice looking. I'd first met him at a good friend's party, and he seemed to take a special interest in me.

We'd kissed once when we were hanging out with friends, swimming in a pool at a hotel where a guy Eric knew worked. I sipped my beer and wondered if tonight would include a second kiss.

A few minutes later, he walked up to me. "Hey, Kristen. How've you been lately? You look really cute tonight. That shirt looks amazing on you."

"Thanks." As he walked away I began to feel lightheaded. I didn't know if it was from talking to Eric or the beer. Maybe both.

There were maybe thirty people at the party, spread out between the upstairs and the downstairs of the house. The hours passed, and we all hung out, listening to music and talking.

A half dozen of us were hanging out downstairs when one of my friends came up to me and squeezed my arm. "Hey, Kristen, we're going to go pick up Jen. She just got off work. We'll be right back."

I nodded. "Okay." My head felt fuzzy, and the room seemed slightly out of focus. I thought about going with them, but the couch was comfortable. I leaned my head back against the couch cushion and closed my eyes. When I opened them a minute later, Eric was sitting in the chair across from me, and we were the only ones downstairs. I wasn't sure if everyone else had left or if they were still upstairs. It didn't matter. I liked Eric. He was always so nice. Ten minutes passed and I rubbed my eyes, trying to focus.

"Where is everyone?" I mumbled to Eric.

"Does it matter?" He moved from where he'd been sitting and was suddenly next to me.

I crossed my arms over my chest, and my stomach tightened. I didn't know what to say or do. I enjoyed hanging out with Eric, but the fact that we were alone together made me uneasy. *Where's Kelley? And everyone else? When are they coming back?* I listened for party noise from upstairs, but there wasn't any. *Surely thirty people couldn't just disappear just like that.*

Maybe we shouldn't be alone. Maybe I should head upstairs.

I pushed my worried thoughts out of my mind and tried to relax. Eric and I chatted about nothing in particular. He was easy to talk to, always polite and respectful. I told myself everything would be fine and that my friends would be back soon, but ten minutes turned into twenty, then thirty.

When are they going to get back? What's keeping them? Did they forget about me?

"Have I ever shown you my movies?" Eric rose and waved me toward his collection.

"Uh, I'm not sure." I felt uneasy but glad for a reason to get off the couch.

Reluctantly, I followed him to the other side of the room. Posters hung on the walls, and his bed sat unmade. On top of his dresser was a stack of music CDs and movies.

"Have you ever seen this movie?" He held up an action flick.

"No, was it good?"

"Yeah. I liked it. Maybe we should watch it sometime."

"Okay."

"Maybe next week."

"Sure," I smiled.

I took a few steps toward the couch, and Eric stepped in front of me, pausing my steps. With a smile, he gently tucked my hair behind my ear. I looked up into his blue eyes, and my stomach danced with nervousness and excitement. Then gently, sweetly, he pulled me close and kissed me. Although surprised, I was okay with the kiss. His lips felt soft. My body relaxed.

We continued kissing, but after a couple of minutes, his kisses grew more intense. It was clear Eric wanted more. His hands groped at me, and I tried to push him away.

I'm not that kind of girl.

"No…wait. Eric…maybe we should go upstairs. Everyone should be getting back soon."

He wasn't interested in talking. His arms pulled me closer. His kisses halted my words. My heart pounded faster, and I pushed against his chest.

Then he took a step, pressing me between him and his bed. I didn't know what to do.

"Eric, no…" I tried to move away from him, but he was stronger than me.

He kissed my neck. His fingers moved to the buttons on my clothes.

"Stop. Don't!"

I pushed his hands away, but he quickly put them back. I tried to push them away again, but his grip tightened. Soon he had the buttons undone.

His arms wrapped around me. My heart pounded faster. Like a wild animal he grunted and pushed me completely onto the bed. It was as if he didn't have any feelings, just desire. I tried to cry out but his mouth covered mine.

"Please, Eric. Don't..."

He continued to undress me.

No!

Again, I resisted, tried to get up...but he pushed me back down and climbed on top of me.

"No. Stop. Please. Get off me!"

My words went unheard. They meant nothing. *I* meant nothing. I froze, fear crippled me, and I couldn't speak.

This can't be happening. This isn't happening.

I felt hot all over, sick, confused. I wanted to cry but tears didn't come.

Get off me! I pushed against him. My body, my heart, ached with pain. I thought I was going to throw up. All attraction for Eric turned to disgust.

Stop, please...

Finally, he pulled back and looked at me. He must have seen horror on my face because his eyes widened and he pushed away. Immediately, he rose and quickly ran up the stairs. I heard him go into the bathroom. My stomach churned, and I thought I was going to be sick.

Distraught, my mind spun with disbelief. I dressed, quietly slipped out, and ran upstairs. I found a phone in the kitchen, yet when I picked it up, I didn't know who to call. I didn't know where my friends were. I didn't know how to reach them.

My parents. I thought about calling them, and tears filled my eyes. If I called them, they'd know I'd been drinking. They'd know I was with older guys.

A new fear tightened the muscles in my shoulders and arms. *If they come they'll know what happened. They'll know I've been raped. Then they'll want to go to the police.* My mind flashed with images of questions and being examined. I didn't want to talk about it.

They could arrest Eric...then there'd be a trial. I pictured a courtroom. The last thing I wanted to do was to sit in front of a roomful of strangers and try to explain what had just happened. Explain the sickening details. All those eyes on me. Shame filled me. I didn't want *anyone* to know. I felt dirty. And worthless.

It's my fault. I shouldn't have been here. I should have gone with my friends.

If I call my parents, they'll know...everyone will know. I didn't want to face that.

Yet I had to get out of there before Eric came back. My heart pounded as I worried that he would find me calling for help. I picked up the phone and called someone from work. Someone who wouldn't ask questions.

The next day when I awoke it was as if I looked through the eyes of a different person. I felt small and powerless, something I'd never experienced before. I'd always prided myself on being a strong, tough girl. I was the girl who sucked it up when I was hurt. The one who didn't cry. And now... I didn't feel like myself at all.

I felt weak, helpless, violated.

I didn't know what to think about the night before. It had all happened so quickly, and I didn't want to believe it was real.

It was just a bad dream. He wouldn't take advantage of me like that. But the images that replayed in my mind and the sinking feeling in my gut told me that it was real.

I can forget it. This won't affect me.

Walking to my job at the pizza place that night, I saw a man striding along the sidewalk toward me, and I felt my body tense. *What if he hurts me?* I looked around, wondering if there was anyone around that I could yell to for help if I needed it.

What's wrong with me? I'd never felt so vulnerable before. *I can't let this affect me.*

The rest of the day, my heart raced at the smallest noises. And as I walked home, it seemed as if the world that had been so bright and happy had darkened into shades of gray. I looked down every street I passed, checking for danger. My eyes darted to every car with fear that Eric would be in one of them.

I'm not worth anything. He never cared. All he wanted was my body. He never liked me. I have nothing to offer anyone else... The thoughts ran through my mind no matter where I was or what I was doing. They drained me. I didn't want to be *that* girl. I didn't want to have these worries. I tried to ignore the images and thoughts that played in my mind—tried to pretend that none of it had happened.

A few days later I was home from school when the phone rang.

"Hello?" I expected the voice of one of my friends on the other end.

"Hey. How are you doing?"

I immediately recognized Eric's voice.

I didn't know how to respond. I was caught completely off guard. "I'm good. How are you?" My hands trembled, and I was afraid to say anything else. I was afraid of letting him know how upset I was. Afraid he'd come and find me.

"You know the other night? Well, I know a lot of people in the police department. If you tell *anyone,* you're going to regret it." Then he hung up.

I pulled the receiver away from my ear and looked at it. *I can't believe he just threatened me.* Anger surged through me, but more than that, fear. Fear that if I told someone it would be my word against his. Fear pushed down my anger over the injustice. *Everyone will believe him, even the police. They know him! They'll make me tell everything, and he still won't be punished. What if he hurts me again?*

I knew at that moment I'd never go to the police. I didn't have the fight in me. The pain was too intense. My emotions were drained from dealing with all the deaths, especially Brandon's suicide. Not telling would be easier than going to court. I was afraid that telling would make Eric angry and he would hurt me again. I pushed all emotions down into a corner of my heart.

It doesn't matter if I don't tell. I don't matter...

The next morning when I woke up, the images of that night were the first thoughts that flashed into my mind. I'd dreamed about it too.

I ignored the thoughts and dreams and rose, feeling like a zombie as I went through the motions. I rubbed my eyes as I got out some cereal. My stomach felt nauseous, and I put the food back.

I usually spent over an hour getting ready for the day, but that morning I didn't. I put on baggy clothes, stuck my hair in a ponytail, and then grabbed my incomplete homework and headed to school, not wanting to go, but not wanting to stay home alone either.

I hated feeling like someone could take advantage of me like that, so I tried to convince myself that we'd had consensual sex. I hoped the lie would take the pain away. I even told one of my friends, hoping that would make it truer. But awake or asleep, honest or dishonest, I couldn't escape the reality that I had been raped.

If you've ever been raped, sexually abused, or taken advantage of in that sort of way…

I am so, so sorry. I know that you can't believe this happened. And I'm guessing that this has made you feel completely taken advantage of and worthless too, but you are worth so much more than you know. God made you perfect and beautiful, and nothing will ever change that. You did not deserve what happened to you, no matter what. Sexual abuse is never the victim's fault.

If you haven't done this already, accept what happened to you and stop keeping it a secret. Please, don't allow this to take more from you than it already has. Tell a good friend, and go with her to the police. If you don't know how you could do that, God will give you the strength. Don't worry. In the end, you will not regret it.

Also, ask God to help you come to the place where you can forgive the person who hurt you. I had to do that with Eric. Forgiveness doesn't mean that what this person did to you was okay, but it is not your job to punish him or her. It's God's. Forgiving that person will help you find freedom and healing so that you can start moving forward with your life. I want that for you.

Love, Kristen

Life

6

I Could Never Do It That Way

Three months later, I still had trouble sleeping and couldn't concentrate on my homework. I'd started throwing up almost daily. Most days I just stared at my backpack without the strength to actually open it, get out the work, and do it. My grades continued to drop.

"Kristen, I need to talk to you about some of your friends," my mom said one evening.

"What about them?" I narrowed my eyes, worried about what she might say.

"I think they're a bad influence on you, honey."

"Why?"

"Well, I didn't think you would ever smoke or drink, but I know that you do sometimes. I don't know if it's peer pressure or what, but I don't like you doing that. You spend all of your free time out with your friends. When you're at home, you're on the phone all night, and your homework isn't getting done. Your grades keep going down. I worry about you, sweetie. I don't know what I can do to help you."

"I know, Mom. None of that's my friends' fault though. I'm not influenced by peer pressure." I acted very confident. I even believed that I was above my friends' influence in many ways, but that really wasn't the case.

"What is it then?"

"I don't know."

I didn't understand my own actions. I knew it was more than my friends' influence, but I had no idea why I was doing the things I was doing. I couldn't bring myself to think much about it. It hurt enough to know that I'd been doing so many things wrong.

"What can I do to help you?"

"I don't know, Mom…" I tried to think of something, but I couldn't think of anything. I wanted to be strong, to take care of myself.

"Okay, Kristen. I'm always here if you want to talk, but if your grades don't improve soon, I'm going to have to limit your time with friends on the weekends and on the phone during school nights. You need to graduate from high school."

"Yeah, I know. I will, Mom, don't worry."

I knew I wasn't doing well in school or in many other ways, but I could hardly worry about it. So many other things consumed my heart and filled my thoughts with worry and pain. I began to live in a fantasy world, hoping and expecting everything would turn out all right in the end.

I understood my mom's concern on some level, but her words had as little impact as my teachers' encouragement had.

"Kristen, I don't understand why your grades are going down," more than one of my teachers had commented. "You used to do so well. It seems like you're not trying."

"I'll try harder," I promised, even though, deep inside, the thought of trying harder seemed impossible. Every time I would open a book, I'd realize I couldn't concentrate on the words or numbers. It was easier to pick up the phone and talk to one of my friends. Often my friends would call for advice. I liked that. I enjoyed listening to them and helping however I could. They were a welcome distraction from all my problems. Still, I always attempted to do better—as if I could force my attitude to change and will all the hard stuff of life to go away.

I pulled out a CD, hoping it would help. "I can see clearly now," sang Jimmy Cliff. Singing along, I raised my voice with the chorus. "It's going to be a bright, bright, bright, bright sunshiny day." That was my favorite part of the song. I sang it as if doing so could change my world.

But even before the song was out of my mind, the tragedies and horror of the past year pushed their way back into my thoughts, reminding me that life was not always made up of bright, bright sunshiny days. Things weren't always right in the world, no matter how much I wanted them to be. Some things were just out of my control.

The darkness hung around, a constant presence. I'd go to work, and people would ask how I was doing.

"I'm here," I'd mumble. That response had become increasingly common. I was there, going through the motions. That was pretty much all my life had become—going through the motions.

A knock sounded on my bedroom door. "Come in," I stated flatly.

The door opened and my mom stepped in. "The doctor called today."

I looked up from the book open on my lap. The book I hadn't been reading. I'd gone through a few dozen tests to find out why I'd been throwing up, including the latest one in which I had to drink some chalky stuff and then have my stomach scoped.

My mom's eyes narrowed with worry. "The doctor said that all the tests came back fine. They say there's nothing physically wrong with you. He thinks it might be psychological."

Confusion filled my mind. "How could that make me throw up every morning?" I leaned back against the wall, tapping my pencil against my book. I hated throwing up. Hated feeling sick. Hated all the appointments. I wished the doctors could find something wrong and give me some type of medication to make it all better. Yet something inside told me this was just one more thing going wrong. That I couldn't stop. One more answer I wouldn't get.

"I don't know, Kristen." Mom opened her mouth and then closed it again, as if not wanting to share the rest of the doctor's news.

"And..."

"And, the doctor suggested you see a psychiatrist. I've already made an appointment. I'll be taking you Tuesday afternoon. You'll have to miss some school."

Not that it mattered. On many days my mom called in to the school for me and told them I was sick. Other times I stayed home whether she gave me an excused absence or not.

"But you'll miss work." My life was messed up. I didn't need to mess up hers too.

"I know, but this is important. I know you've been going through a lot. Things have been hard for you since Brandon's death."

You have no idea... Pain jabbed at my heart, but I refused to acknowledge it. I considered asking my mom how a psychiatrist was different from the counselor she'd brought me to a few times. The counselor had seemed nice enough. She'd asked about everything that was bothering me. I talked to her about all the deaths, especially Brandon's. I also told her about some problems with my friends, issues with my parents, and the unwanted attention of my ex-boyfriend and other guys at school.

It didn't take me long to figure out that the counselor told my mom everything I said. It didn't seem right. After a few weeks my mom didn't hide where she was getting the information. "But Diana said..."

I didn't know what the psychiatrist would do differently, but I could tell from the look on my mother's face that she would continue to press until I agreed to go. Fighting, I'd discovered, was too hard. Instead of arguing with my mom, telling her that I didn't need another person trying to help, I nodded. "Yeah, okay, whatever. I'll go."

"Good. I'll pick you up at school on Tuesday around two o'clock."

I nodded, feeling anxious, surprised, and angry all at once. *Great. This is just what I need. Now I have mental problems too. One more thing to worry about. One more thing to stress out my parents.*

I stared at the ceiling, unfinished math papers lay scattered beside me on my bed. Another assignment I was going to fail. Heaviness settled on my shoulders and pressed down on my chest. *Are things ever going to get better?* Nothing could change what Eric had done. Nothing could bring back the people I had lost: my grandmother…Brandon.

Brandon. I miss him. Why did he hang himself?

Hanging seemed so dramatic, so dark.

During the months after the funeral, I couldn't believe that he actually had killed himself. *I could never do that. I could never commit suicide.* It was too selfish, leaving everyone behind with so much hurt and so many questions. It just wasn't something I was capable of carrying out. But I was beginning to understand why someone wouldn't want to be here. *Life is so hard. This world is so painful and messed up.*

I fluffed my pillow and let my mind wrap itself around everything that had gone wrong in my life. And my thoughts began to change. *If* I ever did commit suicide…I could never do it *that* way.

I knew if I ever made that decision, I'd have to think of some way I wouldn't survive. I knew girls from school who had survived after cutting their wrists or taking pills. They had come back to school with a thousand eyes on them, with everyone knowing what they had done, whispering about it behind their backs and looking down on them. I couldn't imagine the humiliation and shame of having everyone knowing I'd attempted suicide and failed.

Just then, a train whistle blew, echoing through the window. Ricocheting through my room. I lifted my head.

A train. That's one way I'd never survive. The thought was there and then gone.

7

Failing at Life

Tuesday came, and my mom picked me up from school to take me to see the psychiatrist. I wasn't happy.

"How are you doing today?" My mom smiled.

"Fine," I said, smiling back, hoping she'd believe me and take me home instead.

If I had handled myself better lately, we wouldn't be doing this. What's my problem? I don't have mental issues... I know I'm normal.

"We're just going to talk to him and see what he says," my mother said. I could see hope in her eyes, and I quickly looked away. All the things that had gone wrong replayed in my mind. I knew no one could change the past, bring people back from the dead, or stop the pain.

I just need to move forward and be positive.

As I walked from the car into the building, my attitude was optimistic. I believed I could show the doctor and my mom that I really was fine.

The psychiatrist was waiting in a large office.

"It's nice to meet you, Kristen. How are you?" He wore a white coat and sat in a chair across from me.

"I'm good." *Most of the time, right?*

"Your mom tells me that you've been throwing up a lot. Is that true?"

"Yeah..." *Don't tell me it's psychological.*

"Are you tired a lot?"

"Sometimes. I don't sleep all the time or anything." But as I said the words, my body felt weary.

"Is it hard to get up in the morning?"

"Not really." *I don't mind getting up. I just don't know how to deal with my life after I'm awake.*

"Are you unhappy?"

"No, I'm usually a pretty happy person." *So many things have just gone wrong lately.*

I answered his questions quickly, simply wanting to be done.

Then he asked what things had been bothering me lately. *What should I tell him? Where do I start? There's no short answer.* I began to tell him about my friends who'd died, but he seemed to be only half-listening, so I stopped. He didn't respond. Didn't ask more about them or offer any sympathy. Instead he glanced at his watch. "Kristen, you've faced some hard things. I think you're throwing up because of stress and anxiety."

Yeah? Whatever. You don't know the half of it.

"I'm going to prescribe something for you. I think it will help."

Fifteen minutes after I walked into the room, the psychiatrist scribbled on his notepad, ripped a small piece of paper off, and handed me a prescription for an antianxiety and antidepression medication. I took it, thanked him, walked from the room, then handed it to my mom.

My mom made sure I took the medication every day for a month. One day, after I suggested I could take the pills on my own, she handed me the small bottle. "Be sure you take one every morning. If you aren't consistent in how you take them, they won't work."

"Yeah, okay." I agreed, even though I really had no desire to keep taking them. I didn't want to be weak anymore, and when I took the medication, it seemed like I was turning over yet another part of my life.

I hated that I'd been to see a psychiatrist. Only people with serious mental problems saw psychiatrists. Right? I felt like I now had a label on me: "Weak. Not good enough. Not tough enough." My parents, my teachers, the counselor, and now this psychiatrist all knew I was failing at life.

"Did you take your pill?" my mom would ask most mornings as the weeks passed.

"Yes, Mom," I'd answer, even on days I didn't.

"Are you sure you took it?" my mom would ask again before she left for work. "If you don't think it's working, maybe I should talk to the doctor."

I would roll my eyes and walk away. I didn't want to be babied, especially about something that didn't help.

I took the medicine...most days...because I really wanted to be a good kid and I figured it couldn't hurt.

But I saw no improvement. Every morning I'd still wake up with pain in my gut. Eventually, I'd walk from my bedroom to the bathroom and vomit into the toilet, my arms quivering as I held myself over the toilet bowl.

Will anything ever help me get better?

Another month passed, and it was time for a follow-up appointment. My mom seemed anxious for me to see the doctor again. She was worried about how I was doing, that I wasn't taking my medication every day, and that even when I did take it, it was soon gone, in the toilet with everything else.

She went in first to talk to the doctor. After a few minutes, it was my turn to go in. I sat in a chair three feet from where the doctor sat. He leaned forward in his seat.

"How are you, Kristen?"

"Fine."

"Is the prescription working for you?"

"No." I expected that he would ask new questions, that he would try to counsel me. I expected him to help me deal with everything or at least tell me to stop taking the medication. He did neither. Instead, he asked me a few other questions that had nothing to do with the issues I was truly struggling with, then quickly wrote me another prescription. I was confused. I crossed my arms over my chest, making it clear that I wasn't happy and didn't want to be there.

"You know what, Little Miss Defiant, keep this up, and you won't amount to anything. You're going to work at McDonald's your whole life."

I leaned back in my chair, shocked. Part of me rose up inside and revolted. *I can't believe he's saying this. Who does he think he is? He doesn't even know me.*

Looking at the doctor, I thought, *Thanks a lot. You're not helping me. This isn't going to help me. This is a joke.* But I didn't say anything. I just took the prescription and left.

I was silent as I got in the car. I buckled my seat belt and stared out my window as my mom backed out.

She glanced at me. "Kristen, are you okay?"

"No. He said I'm a defiant brat and I'm not going to do anything with my life." Tears filled my eyes. I clenched my teeth and crossed my arms over my chest.

My mom backed the car out of the parking spot. Her hands tightened around the steering wheel.

I could see guilt on her face, as if it were her fault. "Listen, Kristen," my mom glanced over at me. "What he said was wrong. It's not true. I don't agree with that. You're going to be okay, and you're going to do things with your life. Great things." Her face grew red, and she got fidgety. She was mad. My mom didn't get angry often, and in a way her feelings validated mine.

Eventually my eyes couldn't contain the tears. I began to cry because of what had happened and so much more—things I couldn't understand. I rarely let myself cry. I usually tried to hide my feelings and keep everything inside, but this time was different.

The psychiatrist's words made me angry, and another part of me sank inside, as if there were quicksand in my gut and it was pulling down all hope. What if he was right?

What if I am this kind of no-good person he says I am? After all, he is a doctor. What if I don't do anything with my life? What if I'm not good enough to ever be happy?

What if my life does amount to nothing?

Was a life like that worth fighting for?

8

Life

Grounded Until Further Notice

I tucked my hands into my pockets as I hurried from the car to the front door of my house. A Christmas wreath still hung on the door, even though it was now New Year's Day. My heart beat quickly as I walked up the long flight of stairs. My shoes felt as if they were filled with lead, and I wasn't looking forward to the confrontation I knew was to come.

I would be in trouble again, but not because I had skipped a class, ditched school, or left the house without asking. Instead, I'd done something worse—at least my parents would think so. I hadn't come home the night before. I'd ignored my curfew and stayed out all night celebrating New Year's Eve with my friends. I knew my parents would be worried when I didn't come home, but I was hoping to show them I could take care of myself. I knew there would be consequences, but I was past the point of caring. I just wanted to have some fun and not worry anymore about the future or pleasing my parents. I pushed the worry out of my mind, just as I'd done with everything else that weighed on me lately.

Why should I care? I don't have to listen to them, right? I'm almost eighteen anyway.

The hinges squeaked as I opened the front door and stepped inside. My mom stood by the window dusting the stereo system. She turned to me as I entered. I could tell she was worried. Frustrated, too. My eyes met hers, then I quickly looked away.

I stuck out my chin and pretended that what I'd done wasn't wrong, that it didn't bother me. The truth was it did. I'd let my mom down. I'd hurt her. My gut churned as if a dozen rocks rumbled inside. I stood there, frozen, not knowing what to say or do.

She's really not happy with me.

They're going to take my car away.

I've failed again…

"Kristen, do you know what time it is?"

I hesitated. "Yeah, ten o'clock."

"What time were you supposed to be home last night?"

"One o'clock."

"Do you have any idea how worried we were? I was up all night. You could have been dead in a ditch somewhere. I had no idea if you were okay or not. This can't continue."

I wasn't sure what she meant by those words, but I rarely saw my mom this distraught. I felt bad, but I didn't want to deal with it…or with her. I knew she was upset that I'd been out all night, but I was upset that my parents had so many rules for me in the first place. My parents were more protective of me than any of my friends' parents were, and I didn't think it was fair. My mom always wanted to know where I was going, who I would be with, and how she could get a hold of me. She talked to my friends' parents, checked in with my teachers, and had taken me to see a counselor. My friends' parents didn't do any of those things. They let their kids live their lives. I wanted freedom like that.

My dad entered the living room, and I could see the concern and disappointment in his eyes as well. I walked past him, toward my bedroom to put my stuff away. And then I heard my parents talking—about me. About what they were going to do with me. A few minutes later I heard my dad's voice.

"Kristen, can you come here please?"

I went to the dining room where he stood.

"You're grounded until further notice." His voice was stern.

My jaw dropped. "What?" I'd never had a punishment like this before.

"Do you understand?" he narrowed his eyes.

"Dad, you can't do that! That's ridiculous!" Heat rose to my face. My heart pounded in fear. I knew he was serious. The rest of my senior year would be ruined.

"You can't ground me for that long."

"You're grounded until further notice, Kristen." He turned and walked away.

I stomped my foot on the floor, wanting to scream. To cry. To run away. My dad hardly ever got involved in my punishments, and I knew now that he was involved, there would be no discussion. He wasn't going to change his mind.

I hurried to my room, slammed my door, then sank into my bed.

Did they think I wanted things to be this way? I swallowed hard and wished my parents had a better daughter. The thing was, I didn't feel like I could be that better daughter.

I had tried to be better. Most of the time I came home when I was supposed to. I was doing a bit better in school—at least in a few classes. I tried to be pleasant. I tried to ignore what I was thinking and feeling and to act as if everything were okay, but it only worked for so long. Eventually I just couldn't do it anymore and needed a release. I needed to have some fun in my life. It wasn't like I meant to make my parents frustrated, sad, or worried. It was just that sometimes I needed a distraction from the painful mess I hid inside.

A few minutes later, my mom entered my room.

"We're going to take back the presents we gave you for Christmas, Kristen. We're either going to return them or give them to someone who will appreciate them. You need to think about what you've done."

"Someone who will appreciate them?" I pressed my lips together as my heart sank.

Why does she think I don't appreciate my Christmas gifts? What does this have to do with me staying out all night? All *my things?*

"Fine. Whatever." I was too tired to fight.

When my mom left, I rose and shut the door, then collapsed back on my bed. My parents hadn't even given me a chance to explain. They had no idea about all the good choices I'd made the night before. Instead of drinking, I'd stayed sober and had driven everyone else around. I wasn't sleeping with boys or doing anything else stupid.

I lay on my bed, staring up at the ceiling. A feeling of injustice battled against an understanding that I'd failed. Again.

I don't care. It doesn't matter.

Nothing matters.

I'd learned over the last few months that it was easier to try not to care than to feel the pain.

After a few moments, I fell into a restless sleep.

After church the next day, my mom lay down for a nap, and my dad went out to buy a new washer and dryer.

I tried to relax on the couch and watch television, but it was all voices and noise. I was disappointed that Y2K hadn't ended the world. Even though I had doubted it would happen, it had been all over the news. Everyone kept talking about it—scientists, professional people. Surely they knew something, right? With everyone talking about it, I began to consider it as a possibility. A part of me even hoped it would happen.

But Y2K had come and gone, and the world was still there. Nothing changed. *Everyone said the world would end. I didn't think I'd have to face my life anymore.*

I flipped off the television. My mind felt heavy, burdened, stressed.

I grabbed a snack, went back to the couch, and put in the videos from Christmas Eve. I wanted to remember some of the happy moments from last week. I smiled softly as I watched videos of my nephews, Jacob and Noah, opening their presents.

See, life isn't all bad, I told myself. Seeing my nephews grow up was something I could look forward to.

The phone rang, and I answered it. It was Kelley.

"Hey, I was just wondering if you wanted to come over to make gingerbread houses? Liz is coming too."

"Really? I wish… I can't though. I'm grounded again." I talked low so my mom wouldn't hear me from the other room.

"Were your parents upset that you didn't come home last night?"

"Um, yeah. Upset is an understatement. They're taking back all my things from Christmas. And they grounded me *until further notice.* I'm so mad."

"That sucks… Sure you can't come?"

I sat down and leaned back in the chair. "I shouldn't…"

"Hmm… What if you came anyway? It'll be fun. It's not like you could get in any worse trouble, right?" I could hear the hint of a smile in Kelley's voice, and I knew she wasn't entirely serious.

"Yeah, you're probably right. I'll come. I can't drive though. You would have to pick me up down the street so my parents don't see me getting into your car."

"Okay, cool! I'll be there in ten minutes. Love you!"

I grabbed my winter coat and wrote a note to my mom, telling her I was going for a walk. I knew I couldn't get in trouble for that. Maybe by the time I got back, my parents would have rethought my punishment.

I hung out with Kelley and Liz for a few hours, but then I figured I should go home. Liz said she'd drive me.

Once in the car, I began to feel the numbness of my soul. I felt as if I were dead inside. Liz dropped me off down the street from my house. I didn't want to go home. I didn't want to face the same scenes I had the day before. Instead, I figured I could waste some time at the pizza restaurant where I worked. It was only a block away, and I needed to pick up my paycheck anyway. While I was there I bought some cigarettes from a machine in the bar next door, and then I started to walk home. When I crossed the street, I saw the light from our living-room window in the distance. I didn't have the strength to go home yet. Instead of turning left to head home, I kept walking straight toward the park.

I never imagined where I would end up.

Life

9

Kind Words and New Questions

I opened my eyes and tried to adjust to the brightness of the hospital room. It wasn't the room I was used to. Bluish green walls gave it a peaceful feel, and it had a large window and private bathroom. Nurses bustled about their station just outside the door. I tilted my head to the left, noticing an IV by the head of my bed. More machines beeped behind me. I couldn't see them, but I recognized their familiar, low drones. The balloons and flowers were back. My mom was arranging them on the windowsill and on the table by my bed. Cards wallpapered the walls. Their return brought a comfort I hadn't felt in a long time.

A nurse I hadn't seen before walked into the room. I licked my lips and noticed the awful taste of medication.

"Would you like some ice chips, Kristen?"

I nodded. She grabbed a cup near my bed and scooped a spoonful of crushed ice into my mouth. The cold wetness felt good, but I wrinkled my nose. The ice tasted like metal.

"You've been moved from intensive to moderate care, Kristen." My mom's excited voice caught my attention.

"How long was I in intensive care?" My voice sounded gravelly.

"One week."

"Are you kidding? It couldn't have been that long." The idea of that much time passing and my not being aware of it made me uneasy. Had I really been that out of it? I wondered how they could move me to a new room without my knowing it. *Will time continue to pass like this?* I worried that if I fell asleep again, the days and weeks would once again slip by, out of my control.

My mom smiled in the sweetest way. "Honey, you're on a lot of medication. I'm sure it's hard to wake up and realize days have passed. They say you'll start being awake more, so that's a good thing. It means you're getting better."

I attempted to smile back at her, but the pain shooting through my legs made that difficult. Part of me was happy that I was getting better, but not all of me.

I don't want to live my life without my legs. It'll be even worse than it was before.

An ache in my chest grew, so I pushed those thoughts to the back of my mind.

"Look at you. You're doing so much better, sweetheart." My dad beamed as he entered my room, chuckling lightly as he often did when he was happiest. "You're going to be up and around in no time! One day I'll be able to walk you down the aisle," he said, giving me a hug.

My mom, dad, sister, and brother—I discovered—had created their own routine of sorts. They took turns spending time with me on a daily basis. It was amazing how they were able to find normalcy in a situation that was anything but normal.

"Now that you're in moderate care, you can have as many visitors as you'd like," the nurse told me as she hustled around the room, jotting down notes in my chart. She handed me a small cup filled with pills. "Time for your medication."

"What are these?" Even though I was awake, my mind was still foggy, and I wondered if these drugs had anything to do with that.

"Oh, just stuff you need for your body to heal," she responded. "Pain medication, antibiotics to fight infection. Antidepressants."

Antidepressants? Can they give me those without telling me? Do I need them?

Before I could ask about the medication, I noticed Shannon standing at the door. I lifted my eyebrows and smiled.

She walked in slowly, cautiously. "I wasn't sure if you were sleeping."

"No, I'm awake."

"Is it okay if I sit on the bed?" she asked.

"Yeah, of course."

Shannon sat down, bumping the bedside table with her leg as she did. "Oh, I'm so sorry. That didn't hurt you did it?"

I smiled. "No, I'm fine, and I doubt I'd feel it if it did. They're giving me so much stuff for the pain…"

"That's good. I wouldn't want to hurt you."

I seriously doubt anything could hurt worse than what I'm already feeling, I wanted to say but didn't.

"Oh my gosh, you'd never believe what I heard at school today."

Shannon's voice was loud and her gestures big as she told me the latest high school gossip.

High school seemed forever ago. People were still going out, partying. I didn't miss drinking, but I did miss normal life. Everyone else seemed to be doing great—or so it sounded from the way Shannon talked. It was as if Shannon was trying to reassure me that I didn't need to worry about everyone. They were good, I was good, and *life* could be good.

I laughed along with Shannon, thankful to talk about things other than my injuries. The last thing I wanted was to be babied.

I enjoyed this time with my friend, but in a strange way I ached to see Shannon's smile, to hear her laughter. *It would have hurt them so much if I had died. I would have done to them what Brandon did to me—to all of us.*

If only I could have figured out how to deal with all the pain inside before it came to this. I was never trying to hurt anyone, yet I had. Especially myself.

Intense pain throbbed through my legs, and I wondered how long it would be until my medication kicked in. I forced a smile as Shannon continued talking, not wanting her to see my pain. It wasn't easy to hide.

The pain in my legs never stopped, even with medication. At times it would flair up. I had horrible muscle spasms in both legs and phantom pains according to my doctors. It felt as if my legs were still there—twisted, broken. My nerves continued to transmit the same messages of trauma that they had that night, as if they were reliving it. *Something's wrong. Something's wrong. Something's wrong!*

Soon it was time for Shannon to leave. "Thank you so much for coming."

"You're welcome." Shannon gave me a hug. "Everything will work out. God kept you here for a reason."

In the days to come, I heard something similar from nearly every person who visited. "Everything will work out. God kept you here for a reason, Kristen."

I wondered what that could mean.

What reason could he possibly have for me to be here without my legs?

I lay in the hospital bed, and my mom and I watched with wonder the beautiful woman Oprah was interviewing on television. Kelley's mom had mentioned Aimee Mullins—an athlete who had two prosthetic legs.

Aimee walked out on stage, and I could hardly believe it. Her legs looked so real, so pretty. She walked perfectly. My heartbeat quickened.

"Mom, that's what I want! I'm going to get legs like that. Isn't that cool?"

My mom's face lit up as she heard the joy in my voice. "Yes, it will be wonderful, Kristen." We talked for a while about prosthetics, about all the possibilities. Then I heard a familiar, happy voice at the door.

"Knock, knock."

My friend Michelle entered and gave me a tight hug. She radiated energy and joy, just as she always did. "What's new, honey? You look like you're getting better."

"I am. I just watched a video of a woman with prosthetic legs. They looked so real and pretty too. I'll be like that. I'll be able to walk again someday."

Tears filled Michelle's eyes, and she hugged me again. "I'm so happy for you, honey. You deserve all the world has to offer. I'm sure they'll be beautiful and you'll walk great."

Someday...

The following days brought a carousel of visitors. In the evenings, after friends and family went home for the night, I had a few quiet moments to think about everyone's words.

"You don't need your legs."

"Everything will be okay."

"You are so special."

"God loves you."

"God must have kept you here for a reason."

Their words were comforting, but they seemed to come a bit too easy. *How do they know everything will be okay? Have they ever been through anything like this?* Their intentions were good, but I wondered why people had waited so long to tell me. *If they really believe I'm special—and that God has a special plan for my life—why didn't they tell me before? Why did they wait until I'm lying in a hospital bed to tell me how much they love me, how much God loves me?* I had needed to hear that just as much in the past as I did now.

"You are so lucky to be alive, Kristen." This statement caught my attention more than any of the others. I'd heard it often from friends and family members, even a few of the nurses, and it always brought questions. Was I really that close to dying? What would have happened if I had died? Would I have gone to heaven?

I'd asked my mom that last question, and I got the answer I was hoping to hear.

"Yes, of course you would have gone to heaven, Kristen." The look on her face told me she was surprised I'd even asked.

Her assurance brought comfort, but I still wondered what the future held. The thing was, I didn't want to think too hard about what was to come. To think about life without legs.

I wasn't ready for that. Not yet.

10

Settling In for the Long Haul

"Hey, Kristen." A young woman walked into my hospital room, smiling. "I'm here to help you with some exercises."

"Exercises?" I glanced down at my legs. Even in my medicated state, the pain was there—strong, intense, and unrelenting.

"Don't worry, it's for your arms—to strengthen them."

I glanced at my mom, who was perched on the edge of one of the chairs. Her eyes looked tired, but her face was bright, and I knew she took great joy in any sign that I was improving.

"Uh, okay."

The doctor had said something about an occupational therapist. I had just assumed it would be someone who'd help me walk. The thought of walking again made me happy and fearful at the same time. If my legs hurt this much now, what would it be like to wear prosthetics?

"I'm going to show you how to use this band." The therapist put her arms in front of her and grabbed both sides of the thick band. She then stretched it until her arms were fully extended to the sides. "This is one of the exercises. You'll be doing reps of ten." Relaxing it, she handed it to me.

I held the band and stretched it as far as my arms could go. *At least I can use my arms for now. At least I'm not completely stationary.*

"You're doing great, Kristen!" The therapist's voice was enthusiastic. "You have great upper-body strength. I'm impressed!"

I nodded and tried to force a smile.

This is only for now. Next, I'll be working on my legs. Then I'll be walking again. Things will be better then.

I did the reps as she showed me, but only as a way to get me to the next step. I didn't want to consider my life in a wheelchair. This was just a means to an end.

Later that week, I awoke one morning to find a metal bar hanging above my bed. It was in the shape of a triangle, and I wondered what it was for.

I didn't have to wonder for long.

A nurse entered with a wide smile. "Kristen, I'm going to show you how to use the trapeze to lift and move your body. This will help strengthen your arms too."

Inwardly, I winced at the thought of moving that much. Every movement hurt. I tried to smile, determined to make the best of it.

"Let's start with you using the bar as we change your sheets. It'll make it easier and faster."

She got the clean sheets ready. "Okay, Kristen, I'll need you to grab the bar and then lift yourself off the bed a couple of inches."

I wasn't sure if I could do it, but as I grabbed the bar and pulled, I was surprised by how light my body felt. The nurse moved quickly, and then I released, letting myself once again rest on the mattress. The pain didn't disappoint me. It came strong. I blew out a soft, slow breath.

A week later the young therapist came back. "Okay, Kristen, today we're going to show you how to get out of bed and transfer yourself to your wheelchair—using this." She held up a lacquered pine board that looked to be about as long as a pizza box, but a bit narrower.

I hadn't been able to leave my bed since I'd come into the hospital. The idea of it both scared and excited me.

"It's a transfer board." The therapist rolled the wheelchair next to the bed. She lowered my hospital bed so it was level with the wheelchair, then placed one side of the board on the bed and the other side on the seat of the wheelchair.

"Okay. Now, with your arms, you need to scoot your body onto the board and then slide from the bed to the chair. Do you think you can do that?"

I shrugged. "I can try."

"Are you sure?" my mom asked.

I ignored her comment and grabbed the sides of the bed, moving my body onto the transfer board. It was harder than I thought.

My mom watched from the other side of the room. The anxious look on her face reminded me of when I was little and climbed too high on the monkey bars.

Slowly, carefully, I scooted into the chair and readjusted my hospital gown. “Will I always have to use this board thing?”

“Not if you develop enough strength. You’re doing great!” The therapist seemed pleased. I was pleased too. It felt good to be able to not depend on other people.

I felt a sense of accomplishment as I sat there. “How long have you been doing this?” I asked her.

“Do you mean working as a therapist?”

“Yeah.”

“A couple of years.”

“Do you like it?”

“Yes, I like it a lot. I like helping people, seeing them improve. Helping them do things they didn’t think they could do.”

“That’s cool. It’s so nice that you get to help people.” *Maybe someday I’ll find a job where I can help people too.* But first I needed to understand my new world, my new life.

I readjusted my pillow under my head. It was one my mom had brought from home. As the days passed and we all started to understand that we were in this for the long haul, my mom tried to make me as comfortable as possible.

I heard a soft knock on the door, and I readjusted myself on the bed, tucking the blanket—also from home—around me.

“Guess who?” Kelley peeked around the door of my room.

“Hey. What are you up to?” I asked, slightly groggy from the medication.

“Actually”—Kelley strode in with a shopping bag from Abercrombie & Fitch in each hand—“I went shopping…for you.”

"Really?" I smiled, surprised.

"I thought you might be getting tired of those hospital gowns."

Kelley hadn't been there thirty minutes when my mom showed up with bags from Old Navy. She smiled when she saw the things Kelley had brought. "I guess we had the same idea. I got some T-shirts, jogging pants, pajamas... stuff that will be easy to put on and wear."

"That is so sweet." I held up a pink shirt that Kelley had brought. "I love it. You guys are so awesome." I couldn't wait to put the new clothes on.

I held up a pair of long pants. *I should have someone tailor these... cut the legs off for me.*

No, it was as if I was responding to myself. *I'm going to need them full length when I get prosthetics.*

After I was dressed, I felt more like myself. The clothes were an improvement, but I couldn't imagine being pain free and completely comfortable again.

My dad showed up a little while later and joined my mom and Kelley. "Good to see you doing so well, sweetheart. Everyone's been asking about you. They say they've been praying. I've been praying for you too."

His words surprised me. He'd never said stuff like that before. I was encouraged, but it was weird at the same time.

"Thanks, Dad." I didn't know what else to say.

One morning I woke up earlier than usual. I felt hot. The IVs pinched. The tape and bandages on my legs pulled. The idea of getting myself washed up and dressed made me smile.

What will my nurses think if I get myself up and ready before their morning rounds? Before my mom shows up for the day? Will they be mad or happy?

Instead of using the board, I used the strength in my arms to lift my body from the bed to the wheelchair. Thankfully, I didn't fall. I felt pretty accomplished getting myself out of bed.

Maybe I can *do this.*

A problem arose at the sink. Instead of handles, it had foot pedals to turn on the hot and cold water.

Oh no, how am I going to do this? I don't have my feet.

I sighed, and then tried to maneuver the wheels of my wheelchair over the pedals. Eventually I got the right pressure and a good temperature.

I leaned forward to wash my hair, propping myself up slightly with my legs. I got wetter than usual, but I managed to wash my face and hair. Then I dried it and put it up loosely in a clip.

I felt like myself again. It felt good. It was nice to have my hair clean. More than anything, it was nice to have done it myself.

By the time the nurse and my mom arrived, I was sitting in the bed cleaned up and ready for the day.

My mom looked to the nurse, confused. Then she looked to me.

"You're all dressed and ready. Who helped you?"

I smiled. "Nobody. I did it this morning when I got up."

The smile disappeared. My mom's eyebrows furrowed with concern. "You did it by yourself? I don't know if you're supposed to do that." She looked to the nurse.

The nurse winked at me. "It's fine. You go, girl. I knew you could do that. You'll be better in no time."

Later that afternoon, one of the nurse's assistants came to my door. "Kristen, do you want to go for a walk?" she asked.

"A walk?" I glanced at her as if to say, *Are you kidding me?*

"Yeah, I'll push you in the wheelchair. I'll walk you down the halls. Maybe we can even head down to the cafeteria for a snack."

"Sure," I said reluctantly. I wanted to leave my room, but I didn't know what it would be like in a wheelchair. As gingerly as I could, I moved from the bed to my wheelchair. My pain was worse after moving around so much in the morning. She took the handles and pushed me out the door into the hall.

The first thing I noticed was that, instead of seeing people at eye level, I was now lower than everyone else. I felt small, weak, helpless. *I hate this.*

I also didn't like the idea of someone pushing me, but I didn't tell the nurse that. A part of me even scolded myself. *I should be appreciative, thankful for her help.*

We paused in front of the elevator, and the nurse's assistant pushed me straight inside, facing the back wall. Other people had entered behind me, but I couldn't see them.

"Uh, can you turn me around? Why am I facing the wall?" My voice was curt, but at that moment I didn't care. I felt less than human, as if I were a lesser member of society. Of course, with an elevator full of people, there was no way she could turn me around. The wheelchair would hit everyone if she tried. Instead, she mumbled an apology.

Even though the ride to the cafeteria only lasted a few seconds, I felt like I was being punished for not having my legs. It was a loss of independence and pride. Sitting inside the cafeteria, I looked outside through the many windows. It was strange that the world was still out there, without me.

I'm still me. I'm still human, I told myself. *Do other people see me differently?*

[illegible]

[illegible]

you must lower [illegible]

[illegible]

We [illegible]

[illegible]

[illegible] was no way the [illegible]

[illegible]

11

Life

The Psych Ward

My dad's face suggested he had something to tell me. "Kristen," he began, as he approached my bedside. "Your mom and I have been talking to the doctors, and they don't think they can do anything else for you here. They're recommending we take you to another hospital."

"What do you mean?"

"Well, now that you are stable, you're going to need to have some surgeries that will prepare your legs for prosthetics, and they can't do those here."

"Why can't they do it here? I like it here." The idea of leaving this place, moving to a different hospital with different people caused a pain to spread from the pit of my stomach.

"Sweetheart, I've done the research. It's a bigger hospital where they can give you more help. The social worker says you need to go, and we've already made the arrangements."

"It's a hospital in Chicago," my mom told me later that day.

"When do I go?"

"In about a week. They'll be taking you in an ambulance. It's about an hour away."

I wanted to ask why I couldn't just go home, but I knew that wasn't an option—not yet.

The day came for me to be transported, and the nurses gave me extra medication to make the ride easier. They wheeled my bed down to the garage level, and then they transferred me to a stretcher in the back of an ambulance.

"Mom, are you coming with me?" I reached out my hand toward her.

"Yes." She climbed in and sat next to me. "Don't worry. I'm here." My quickened heartbeat slowed. "Dad's following in the car. He'll meet us there."

In the back of the ambulance, the sides seemed too tight, too close. As I lay there, strapped to the stretcher, I thought back to the night of my rescue. It had been six weeks since the train ran over me, and I still wasn't sure what had happened. All I remembered was the pain, the anger, the fear. How I had wanted my life to end.

I pushed all those thoughts out of my mind and tried to keep myself calm. I breathed in and out slowly, wincing at every bump. Finally, it came to the point where I couldn't distract myself from the pain, and tears came.

My mom clung to my hand. Tears filled her eyes.

"If I could, I'd take the pain for you, sweetheart." She swallowed hard, and I believed her.

We eventually arrived, and they rolled me into an intake room.

"I thought you said her room would be ready." I heard my mom talking to a nurse.

"Soon… I'll let you know."

Confusion filled my mind. "Mom, why isn't my room ready? Didn't they know I was coming?" My mom hesitated and let out a heavy sigh.

I searched her eyes, wondering what had her so bothered.

"Before you can be admitted into the regular hospital, you'll have to stay in the psychiatric department. They want to do some tests. Don't you remember?"

What? I don't remember. The psych ward? Do they think I'm crazy? They must really believe I did this to myself if I have to go there.

I nodded, mostly because I didn't know what else to do. *Don't worry, Kristen, the sooner you get through it…the sooner you'll get the surgeries…the sooner you'll be walking.*

As I waited, I imagined all the places I'd seen in movies. Men and women with messy hair, wearing straitjackets, pounding their bodies against the padded cells, peeing on themselves.

I'm not crazy. Why are they making me go there?

I looked down to where my legs used to be. *Of course they want me there. They think I tried to kill myself.* For weeks I'd thought only of getting better. *Now…now I'm going to have to face that they think I did this to myself.* I still wasn't sure whether or not I had.

Even though my stomach felt queasy at the thought of being there—

and even though I still worried about what I'd find—I made a vow to cooperate as best I could. I'd show them. I'd prove that I was in my right mind.

A nurse pushed my wheelchair through the hospital. My parents followed behind.

As we entered the psychiatric department, I became apprehensive. It was in a much older part of the hospital. I looked back at my parents, and I could see the apprehension on their faces as well.

The nurse wheeled me toward my assigned room, and the eyes of the other people in the unit followed.

The walls were dingy, and a sour smell hung in the air. The large room looked like something from a 1950s horror flick. There were two hospital beds—crank beds—very different from the electric ones I had at the other hospital.

This can't be where they meant to bring me.

A nurse handed me a yellow folder with my name on it. "This is the information on our program and the rules you need to follow during your stay with us. Please read through everything while I talk to your parents." After I figured out how to wheel myself to the side of my bed, I opened the folder, took out a packet, and read:

> **Adolescent Psychiatry Program**
>
> Our program is a specialty care program designed to meet the needs of the adolescent. The treatment team is composed of psychiatrists, registered nurses, mental health workers…

I scanned the rest of the page.

The safety and well-being of patients, family and staff is of primary concern. When you visit our unit, please sign in and out. Staff must check all items—packages, personal belongings and gifts. Those items that do not meet "safe" will be placed in the adolescent's "Belongings" cabinet…

Visiting Hours, Monday–Friday, 7:30 p.m.–8:30 p.m.

I turned the page over.

Unit Rules

The following behaviors are not allowed:

Physical aggression or physical contact

Destruction of property

Verbal threats or verbal aggression

Gang colors, indicators of gang affiliations or organizations

Gang signs

Clothing with drug/liquor/violence/racist themes

Exposed tattoos

Jewelry including earrings and any body piercing objects

Exchange of gifts between patients

Swearing or obscene language

Sharp or dangerous objects

Food and drink in patient rooms

Visiting in patient rooms

Visitation or contact with hospitalized patients following discharge

Room searches will be conducted daily and as needed.

I put down the packet, wanting to cry. *Where am I?*

As if in answer, a nurse's assistant came to check my things.

"We'll have to take the strings out of your hoodies," she said. "I'll have to take your makeup, blow-dryer, and curling iron. If you need those things, you must ask for them, and someone will stay here with you as you use them." She looked through all my items, and I realized she was looking for anything I could use to hurt myself or someone else.

Afterward, my parents came to hug me good-bye. They weren't allowed to stay any longer, but they promised me they would be back as soon as they were allowed. "We're talking to the staff about the visiting hours. We think it's too soon for you to be alone so much of the time."

The first few days were hard. In the other hospital my days had been filled with visitors. People could call me, and I could call them anytime. All that had changed. Only family could visit me now. They got to stay longer than other people's guests, but they couldn't stay all day anymore.

One evening I rolled my wheelchair out to the common area.

"What happened to you?" one woman asked as she looked at my legs. Her eyes were wide, curious.

I didn't want to talk about why I was there or my injuries. Then again, I wanted this woman to know I hadn't always been like this—that I'd been a whole person once.

"Uh…," I hesitated. "I got run over by a train."

She nodded but didn't answer, then turned her attention back to the television.

The next day one of the counselors approached me, holding out his hand. "I'm Nester." He was tall and stocky with a short beard. He wore a button-up plaid shirt with his name tag clipped to his pocket.

"Hi." I reached to shake his hand. "I'm Kristen."

He sat down beside me.

"How are things going?"

"Pretty good, it's just..."

"It's just what?"

"Everyone keeps asking me what happened."

He nodded, and I assumed he knew what happened.

"So what do you tell them?"

"That I got run over by a train."

"That sounds to me like the right thing to say."

"I don't need to tell them details?"

"No, they don't need to know."

"Good, because I don't remember much." I wanted to tell him that everyone said that I'd attempted suicide, but that I wasn't sure I had. It had been six weeks since the train ran over me, and I still had no idea what had happened.

"I don't like talking about it," I added.

Nester focused on me. "I'd probably feel the same way. Do people think you did it on purpose?"

"Yeah, they do. But I don't think I could have done that..." I let my voice trail off.

"Just keep thinking about it. Take one day at a time. You'll figure it out. People who love you will still love you. You just need to be happy you're still here."

"Yeah…I am."

It was nice having someone to talk to.

Across the room a man spun in circles, repeating over and over, "I want to go home. I'm hungry."

Nester turned to him. "You're fine, Joe. Everything's cool."

I smiled, thankful I didn't seem to be as bad off as some of the other people around there. I felt bad for them, but they actually made me feel more normal than ever.

That night, the pain was worse than usual.

"Don't worry, honey," said a nurse, as she stroked my hand. "They're experimenting with your medication… It'll be better soon."

Soon I should be released. Then the doctors can do the other surgery. I'll be able to start walking again. I didn't want to mess that up. Still, it was hard not to be scared or sad, especially since I didn't have as many distractions, which meant the memories of that night surfaced more and more. As much as I tried to figure them out, none of the memories included how I got onto the train tracks.

"Kristen, time to change your bandages," the nurse said, as she whisked into my room. This would be the second time she changed them that day. Lately, it seemed my legs were bleeding more, even though it had been eight weeks since I'd lost my legs. My parents wondered if the bleeding was caused by my increased activity. I wasn't getting the same level of attention as I'd had at the previous hospital, and I had to do a lot more for myself.

Most of the time I didn't watch when the nurse changed my bandages.

But this time I paid attention. As she unwrapped them, I was shocked by how ugly the wounds still looked. What stood out to me the most were the stitches. Hundreds of them—big, thick, long, black. They were in every direction, covering every inch. I knew the doctors had done the best they could to save my life, stop the blood flow, and mend what had been left of my legs. Still, it wasn't pretty.

There was a huge area on the left side of my knee where my skin looked like black leather. The tissue had died, and it was going to have to be cut out during my next surgery. I wasn't looking forward to it.

"You're going to have to learn to do this yourself," the nurse told me. "You'll need to learn how to change your dressings and care for your wounds before you go home."

"I'm going home?" I felt my heartbeat quicken.

"Yes. I heard the doctor saying that you're being discharged soon. Won't it be good for you to go home for a few days—before your next surgery?"

"Yeah…"

Home. It seemed like something from a dream. I couldn't imagine really being there. It had been two months. So much had happened since the last time I'd walked out those doors. *Will everything still be the same?* I assumed it would be.

Everything except me.

[illegible]

[illegible]

[illegible]

[illegible]

[illegible]

[illegible]

[illegible]

12

Life Facing New Challenges

"Okay, Kristen, the paperwork is done. We can go out now."

I nodded as the nurse pushed me to the front door of the hospital. My mom walked beside us. As we approached the large glass doors, I could see my dad was already in the driveway, parked right in front of us.

The automatic doors opened, and the fresh air rushed toward me—the first fresh air I'd breathed in months. The Chicago wind whipped my hair around my face as the nurse pushed me to the car. Until that day, I had taken fresh air for granted my whole life.

The nurse rolled me to the car. *How in the world am I going to do this?* I had been taught how to transfer from a bed to my wheelchair, but no one had worked with me on how to transfer from my wheelchair into a car. The distance seemed impossible.

I looked to my parents and the nurse. They seemed as ill-prepared as I was. Tension tightened my shoulders, but I ignored it and grabbed the door handle with my right hand and the top of the seat with my left.

"Here, let me help." My dad reached down and grabbed my waist from behind, lifting me. I also pushed up with my arms, and he guided me to my seat.

My body was tense as cars zoomed past us on the busy interstate. My heart pounded in my chest, and worries pounded in my head. *What if we get in an accident? Will I get hurt? Would I be even worse off than I am now?* An ache in my chest told me I didn't want to experience that type of trauma again.

I sat quietly in the car, watching out the window and counting the minutes until we got home and I was no longer in danger.

As we turned onto the street where we lived, new tension filled me when I saw the park and the railroad tracks. My fists clenched on my lap as the car went over the tracks. With the *clunk-clunk* of the tires passing over the rails, my mind filled with images of that night, but I quickly pushed them away. I didn't want to think about what had happened. I felt sick in the pit of my stomach. I averted my eyes and focused on the two-story brick building.

Home.

Dad parked in front of the house. My brother had recently moved back home to help my parents take care of me, and my mom went upstairs to get him. A minute later Ryan came to the side of the car.

"Hey, how's it going?" My brother smiled, acting as if my needing his help to get into the house was the most natural thing in the world. "It's a beautiful day outside, isn't it?"

"Let's see how we can get you inside." He eyed me for a moment, then leaned into the car. "Okay, wrap your arms around my neck, and I'll just lift you up."

I did as he asked, and a few seconds later I was in his arms. Though I was relieved to be out of the car, the movement brought lightning bolts of pain. I winced and bit my lower lip, not wanting Ryan to notice. He had been careful. It wasn't his fault it hurt.

He carried me up the sidewalk and to the front door. My brother had given me piggyback rides while I was growing up, but he'd never carried me like this before. That he had to do so now felt humbling and awkward. Neither of us spoke.

Inside the building, a tall set of stairs rose straight up and then turned and wrapped around, leading to our home on the second story. As Ryan carried me up and put me on the couch, I had a sinking feeling. *Will I ever be able to walk up the stairs again on my own? Will I always need someone to carry me?* I felt so helpless.

Ryan brought my wheelchair up to the living room, and I transferred into it. But when I unclamped the brakes and started to wheel, I knew immediately there was a problem. I tried to roll over the thick, plush carpet, but the wheelchair hardly moved an inch.

At the hospital, the carpet in the halls was thin—easy to roll over. Now I pushed and pushed, and still I couldn't move very fast. My arms burned and shook. My muscles tightened.

I can't believe I can't do this.

I took a deep breath and tried harder. With great effort I wheeled myself to my room. The chair scraped the doorway and the door as I entered.

"Sorry," I glanced back over my shoulder. My parents and brother were all watching me. I could tell my mom was worried that I might be feeling guilty.

"Don't worry about the paint, Kristen." My dad smiled. "It's fine."

My room looked mostly the same, though neater than I remembered. I figured my mom had cleaned while I was gone. I turned around and went back into the kitchen. As soon as I reached the wooden floor, I could roll easily again.

I wheeled to the cabinet to get a glass for some water. The cabinets were high, and I was low. After stretching to reach a glass, I rolled to the fridge, but I didn't know how to open it with my wheelchair in the way.

"Oh honey, I can do that for you. What do you want?" I could tell my mom hated seeing me struggle.

My mom got a pitcher of water, and after I drank the water, I decided to use the bathroom. Again everyone followed me. It was as if we were on an exploratory adventure together.

I got to the bathroom and tried to roll inside, but the back wheels of my chair hit the door frame. The doorway was too narrow for my chair to fit through. I heard a thump, followed by the cracking of paint and wood.

Fear gripped my chest. *How can I live here if I can't use the bathroom?*

"Oh honey, is the doorway too small?" Mom looked to my dad. "We're going to have to get that adjusted."

Ryan stepped forward. "What do you need me to do?"

"We'll think of something." My dad's voice sounded desperate.

"I don't really have to go." I turned around and moved back to the living room. My efforts seemed even harder with the weight of worry upon me.

"I think I'll lie down," I said to Ryan, who'd followed me.

"Here, I'll help you." He eased me onto the couch.

Everyone was trying hard to act like everything was normal, which almost made things worse because everything was so *not* normal.

My mom walked into the room and smiled. "Time for your medicine."

I was thankful. Thankful for the pain relief—and for the sleepiness that would take me away from all these problems.

When I woke up I saw they'd taken off the bathroom door and hung a curtain in its place.

Life as I had known it was over; so much would never be the same.

"How are you feeling?" Stacey's voice was pleasant as she walked through the door carrying Noah. My nephew Jacob followed close behind. I'd been home a couple of days, and she knew I was eager to see them. "Is it good to be home?"

"Yeah. Things are just...different."

I stretched out my hand and stroked Noah's soft hair.

Stacey smiled, trying to be encouraging. "It's okay, Kristen. I'm sure you'll get used to it."

My stomach ached at her words. *You have no idea. You don't know how hard this is. You've never lost your legs. You can walk up stairs and walk on carpet.*

Four-year-old Jacob was standing on the other side of the room, looking at me. He seemed to have grown at least two inches during my time in the hospital.

"Come here." I patted the couch beside me.

He stood there, staring at me. I could almost read the expression on his face. He was used to me chasing him and carrying him around on my shoulders. I could tell he was confused.

Finally, a few minutes later, Jacob approached and sat next to me with his toys. We both knew it wasn't the same.

After they left, I felt tired of just sitting in my chair or lying on the couch and decided to move to the floor. I took a breath and pushed off the couch with my arms. Stretching out my right leg, I pressed it to the floor, bearing all of my weight on the end where it had been severed. Waves of pain ran up my leg as it slid away from the couch; then I slowly lowered my body the rest of the way to the floor so I wouldn't fall.

"Be careful. You're going to hurt yourself. Just take your time. We're not in a hurry," my mom said to me. She'd been saying things like that ever since I came home.

She spoke the words, but I could tell my dad thought the same things. He watched in silence, and I couldn't help but be annoyed with them both.

You're overreacting. Do you want me to depend on other people forever?

"Are you hungry?" my mom asked later that evening, after I got up from a nap. It bothered me that I felt so tired all the time, that I had to take naps.

"No, I'm going to sit out back."

My mom followed me as I opened the door and rolled my wheelchair onto the back porch. It was closed in and heated. Two stories up, the porch overlooked our yard and the car lot next door. I could see the railroad tracks in the distance. I wanted to go outside but could only go down as far as the first step. I hated feeling so restricted. I lit up a cigarette, not caring if my mom—or anyone else—saw me or disapproved. I took a puff and blew it out slowly, wishing I could blow out all the tension built up inside as easily.

How am I going to live my life like this?

Somehow prayers mixed with my thoughts.

God, why did you let this happen? Why did you keep me here without my legs?

Memories of all the physical things I'd done ran through my mind. Images of me playing soccer and volleyball in the backyard. Images of me running up and down the stairs of our house and of Ryan teaching me how to ride my bike in the parking lot next door.

There is no way I'll be able to do any of that anymore.

Emotion built within me, but I was too heartbroken to cry.

I can't do anything. I can't even leave my house. My life really sucks now.

Why did everyone always tell me that God had saved my life? That he had rescued me for a purpose? Was that nice of him? or cruel? Was life without my legs a punishment somehow?

God, why didn't you just let me die?

As the minutes ticked by, my will to live weakened. I continued to think about the things I could no longer do. Running. Playing on the swing set in our yard. Jumping from the railing of our back porch onto the roof of the building next door. Tears filled my eyes. I hated that I couldn't ever do them again, even if I wanted to.

Why do I have to be here? Why do I have to live my life like this? Is it always going to be this hard? My arms ached. My legs ached. My heart ached.

I thought things were bad before, but I never realized how good I had it.

Stupid teenage girl. Why didn't you believe things would get better? Even though I didn't fully believe it, I suspected that I really had tried to commit suicide. It was the only thing that made sense.

13

Life

A New Reality

Sunlight streaming through my bedroom window interrupted my dreams. Ten seconds before, in my dream world, I was at high school with my friends, talking and laughing as we strode through the halls.

I brushed my hair from my face and rubbed my eyes. *Today is...Sunday. Yay! No school today.* I smelled my dad's coffee and could hear my parents talking in the kitchen.

Opening my eyes, I looked to the window and then toward the doorway. That's when I spotted it. A wheelchair. In an instant, memories of everything that had happened came flooding back and slapped me in the face. My heart dropped.

Welcome to reality.

"Kristen, time to get up." My mom entered the room. "Do you need help getting ready for church?

You want me to go to church?

Just thinking about it made me tired. It was so hard to get up, to move. It hurt to ride in the car. Didn't they know how hard it would be for me to get there?

"Mom, I'm not sure. Do we have to go today?" I knew my parents would help me, but I didn't want to depend on them, and there would still be a lot I had to do for myself.

"Yeah, we need to go. It will be good for us. There are a lot of people there who'll want to see you."

"Fine." I sat up in bed, still unsure whether it was a good idea.

An hour later, we drove up a hill to our church. My parents helped me into my wheelchair.

The church's large doors faced the parking lot, and as I wheeled closer I noticed there was a step leading up to the doors.

Great. Here we go again.

One thing was for sure, I couldn't get into church on my own.

I rolled up to the step and paused. It was as if one hundred steps were stacked in front of me. I again felt powerless, weak.

"You get one side of the wheelchair, I'll get the other," my dad told my mom. Then they lifted me up the small curb.

My sour attitude changed as I saw everyone inside smiling at me. Many of these people had sent me cards and flowers in the hospital. My mom said they'd also made meals and sent money in case we needed it.

After the service many people approached me and took my hands in theirs, patted my shoulder, and gave me hugs.

"It's so good to see you."

"We're happy you're still here."

"You look beautiful today, Kristen."

Their evident love for me felt good. I felt normal, like I belonged.

After most of the people had left, my parents were still talking to some of their friends. I knew I couldn't go down that step to the parking lot alone, so I waited near a corner of the foyer.

A woman I'd never seen before approached me. She wore a solid red dress. She was tall, thin, and her brownish gray hair was pinned up. Soft bangs framed her face. I looked up at her and smiled, expecting to hear the same things I'd heard all day.

"It's a good thing your suicide attempt didn't work," she said. "You would have gone to hell if you'd died."

I didn't know what to say—how to respond—so I just sat there. What surprised me was she said it so matter-of-factly, as if she were telling me the sky is blue.

And then she turned and walked away. My jaw dropped as I watched her go.

Who does this woman think she is? I'm a good person. Everyone says I would have gone to heaven.

But fear crept into my mind. *What if what she said is true? What if I would have gone to hell?*

I looked around, wondering if I should ask someone. Everyone was involved in other conversations.

Did that woman say that because she believed everyone who commits suicide goes to hell? I've heard some people believe that. Or does she think I'm a bad person? She doesn't even know me.

My parents approached with smiles on their faces. “Ready to go, darling?” my dad asked.

I nodded, and they helped me into the car. It was only as I sat in the backseat on our way home that I dared to speak up.

“Do you know that lady who came up to me after church?”

“What lady?”

“The one in the red dress. I don’t think I’ve seen her before.”

“I don’t know. I’m not sure,” my mom said. “There were a lot of people… Why?”

“When I was sitting in the foyer, she told me I would have gone to hell if I had died.”

Both my parents were silent, and then my dad spoke up. “Who is this woman? Why would she say that?” Anger laced his words.

“Kristen, of course you would have gone to heaven,” my mom assured me.

“But Mom, what if—”

“No, no, you would have gone to heaven, sweetheart.” My mom reached back for my hand and held it in hers. “Don’t worry about what she said. We’re just glad you’re still here.”

I wished I could believe her. Instead, a heaviness settled over me. Tears rimmed my eyelids. I knew I should have died, and more than anything, I wanted to know where I would have been right then if I had. Heaven or hell?

Monday morning when I arrived back at the hospital, familiar sterile scents greeted me. My mother held my hand as the nurse took my stats in preparation for surgery. Fear tightened around my chest, but I ignored it. I wasn't looking forward to the surgery and recovery, but I knew it would be worth it.

It's going to help me walk better on prosthetics. I can't wait. I hope it won't be long. I hope the prosthetics don't hurt too much and that they look real, like the ones in the video. Maybe things will be normal again once I have those.

"I'll see you when you get out. We'll all be praying everything goes well." My mom offered a slight smile, but I could see worry in her eyes. They wheeled me back to surgery, and as I stared at the tiles on the ceiling—tiles and lights, tiles and lights—I thought back to when they brought me to the emergency room on that cold January night. I wanted to die then. And now? I wasn't sure.

Waking up from the surgery, I felt the kind of pain I'd felt those first days in the hospital. The pain was the same, maybe worse. I tried to be positive, but the medication once more made my mind cloudy, and I felt sapped of energy.

The days passed, and I enjoyed the visits from friends and the letters and cards I received. Still, I didn't know what to think of my future.

It has to get better. It can't get too much worse than this. It has to get better. Or will it?

Even though I tried to think positively, I found myself beaten down, exhausted, depressed. The nightmare wasn't ending. *This is reality.*

No matter how positive I tried to be, I knew my life would be different. *How will I live? How will people view me? What kind of a daughter, friend, aunt, sister, and mother will I be now?*

Weeks had passed, and recovery was more of the same. Looking for a distraction, I popped in a CD that a friend had brought me. A song caught my attention, and I played it over and over again.

"Hey, Mom, listen to this," I told her the next day when she came to visit. The melody filled the room, and I smiled.

"There's a light in me, that shines brightly. They can try, but they can't take that away from me," Mariah Carey sang.

The song continued, and the messages of not being afraid and refusing to lose faith in dreams resonated in my heart. As I listened, my perspective shifted. Maybe things really could be different. Better, even.

Hope was a welcome song in my heart.

I had only been home from the hospital a few hours when the phone rang.

"Hello?"

"Hey, Kristen, it's Shannon. I was wondering if you wanted to go out tonight? A few of us are going to a party."

"Yeah, okay. Sure."

After I hung up, I was excited about the idea of going to a party, but I worried about what everyone would think. What would people say when they saw me without legs? Could I really just go out and enjoy myself like I used to?

I was looking through my closet, trying to find cute clothes to wear, when my mom entered.

"Going somewhere?" she asked. Though she tried to act casual, I could hear the tightness in her voice.

"Yeah, Shannon's coming to pick me up. We're going out with some friends."

My mother's brow furrowed. "Do you really think that's a good idea?"

"Yeah. Why not?"

"I'm not sure, Kristen. Your leg hasn't really healed from surgery. What if you bump it? You just had major surgery. You need time to heal."

In my mind's eye I could see the thick black stitches that were on my thigh where they'd removed a muscle and moved it to the bottom of my leg. I could picture the skin graft, where they'd replaced the dead tissue on my knee with some skin from the back of my leg. But unlike last time I was home—when I worried about not being able to live a normal life—this time I wanted to prove to myself and everyone else that I *could* live a normal life. I wanted that more than anything.

"I'll be fine. I'll be careful. I won't stay out too long."

"So how are you going to get around?" She folded her arms over her chest.

"I don't know. We'll figure something out."

When Shannon arrived, I scooted down the long set of stairs on my butt. After I reached the bottom, Shannon did her best to help me maneuver out the front door and down one more step with my wheelchair. She was patient while I got in and out of her car, but I was disappointed when we got to the party and I realized it was in an upstairs apartment.

Shannon must have seen the discouraged look on my face.

"Don't worry. We'll get up there." She parked the car and ran around to the passenger side. "Why don't I give you a piggyback ride, then come back for your wheelchair?"

I was still worried what people would think about my being in a wheelchair, but I tried not to think about it. Shannon gave me a piggyback ride to the top of the stairs, then knocked on the door.

"Come in," we heard a voice call from inside. The door opened, and a sea of faces greeted us.

"Hey, Shannon. Hi, Kristen. It's great to have you here."

Shannon put me down on the sofa and went back for my wheelchair. For a moment I forgot that things were different.

"Good to see you, Kristen."

"I really like your hair that way."

"It's so good to have you around again. We missed you."

All the time I was in the hospital, this is all I ever wanted—to be normal. Yet I realized that being normal wasn't what I'd been missing. I was out with my friends again, yet something still didn't seem right.

I tried to enjoy the time with my friends, but after a while I noticed people who didn't know me very well looking at me. Actually, they weren't looking at *me.* They were looking at my legs. Seeing the curiosity on their faces made my stomach tighten.

That's the first thing people are going to notice, I realized. I didn't want to be defined by my injuries. More than that, the party didn't seem to be as much fun as I remembered.

Maybe there is a lot more to life than just having fun or partying and drinking.

It seemed as though everyone at the party was having fun, but I saw an emptiness in their faces. They were looking for happiness but not really finding it. I felt sad for them, yet I envied them at the same time. *They don't realize how much they have. They don't realize their potential and all they can do.*

I felt more and more unsettled. I wanted and yearned for something much more, something much deeper. The real meaning and point to life. Everything I had longed for now seemed so small, so minor and pointless.

When it was time to go, we used the piggyback method again. We were almost to the car when I felt myself slipping from Shannon's back. I felt helpless as I tumbled to the ground. Pain shot up my legs.

"I'm so sorry!" I could see by Shannon's expression that she felt bad. I tried to laugh, but tears filled my eyes.

"Can you, uh, help me..." Heat rose to my cheeks.

I can't believe this is happening. I can't even get myself off the ground. I really can't. This is horrible.

Shannon looked at me wide-eyed, and I followed her gaze. Blood was seeping through my jeans.

I winced.

"Oh, Kristen... I'm so sorry."

I forced a laugh, trying to pretend it didn't hurt. "I'm fine, really. Please, don't worry."

When I got home that night, my mom immediately noticed the blood on my jeans.

"Kristen, I thought you were going to be careful."

"I was being careful, Mom. I'm sorry. I'm fine."

The next day after a shower, I found a note waiting on my pillow:

Dear Kristen,

It seems like when I try to talk to you about your surgery and taking care of yourself, you get upset. I'm very worried about the bleeding. You had a very long and delicate surgery just a few days ago. Please promise me you'll call for help when you need to transfer from the floor. Your knee is in a very delicate healing stage right now and can't support your weight in getting down from your chair or in pulling or pushing you back up to your chair. I just need you to take everything a little slower than you have been.

I love you so very much. There will be lots of time to do more things once you are healed. Please know I'm not trying to hold you back in any way.

All my love, Mom

My shoulders tightened as I read the note. I knew my mom only wanted what was best for me, but I thought she'd understand more than anyone. I just wanted to keep up with everyone around me. I just wanted to be normal.

But deep down, there were also things I was trying to run away from.

Life

14

A Second Chance

The doorbell rang, and my mom went downstairs to open the door and invite a young couple in. Large smiles filled their faces as they entered the living room.

"Hey there!" Val, my physical therapist, walked in and gave me a hug. She and her husband, Brad, lived in Stacey's neighborhood and were friends with my sister. Stacey had arranged for them to come to the house for dinner so we could all get to know one another better. "How are those stretches going?" Val asked.

I smiled back, laughing to myself. *Even on our day off, she's still asking about stretches.* "They're going pretty good."

"Awesome. Keep it up."

Brad walked over and shook my hand. "Hi, Kristen, it's really nice to meet you. How have you been? We've been praying for you a lot."

"I've been doing good, thank you." I felt a bit shy. People often told me they prayed for me, which I appreciated, but I still felt a little uncomfortable.

"Thanks for having us over," Val said, turning to my mom.

"We're so glad you're here." My mom's face beamed.

After dinner, we moved into the living room. My mom and I sat on one couch, while Brad and Val sat on the other couch nearby. My dad and Ryan pulled up chairs.

"It's such a blessing you're still here," Val said. It was a simple statement, but one that put me on edge. My throat felt dry, and my hands fidgeted on my lap. *What if I wasn't still here? What if I had died that night? What if that woman was right? Would I have gone to hell? This is too important for me not to have an answer.*

Straightening my back, I looked at Brad. "Do you think I would have gone to hell if I had died?" I'd heard from my sister that Brad was going to a Christian graduate school in the area to become a pastor, so I really wanted to hear what he had to say. I felt that, of all the people I knew, he could tell me what the Bible says about heaven and hell and who goes there. More than anything I wanted to know the truth. I needed to know the truth. I didn't think Brad would just tell me something that would make me feel better, and he didn't.

I could see that Brad was taken aback by my forwardness. He straightened and took a deep breath. "Well, the Bible says you have to ask Jesus to forgive you of your sins and to come into your heart. It's only then—once you've accepted him—that you will go to heaven."

I hesitated. "So, how do you know if you've ever asked Jesus into your heart? I mean, I've always believed in God, and I know that Jesus is the Son of God, but I don't think I've done that," I hurriedly continued. "I've gone to church my whole life, but I've never heard anything like this in church before... I mean, isn't it good enough to just know who Jesus is?"

"Actually, just knowing isn't enough." Brad spoke with tenderness and kindness. "God is perfect, holy, and just. He created all of us to be in a personal and intimate relationship with him, but because of our sin and the wrong things we've done, we are separated from God forever. That is why he sent his Son, Jesus, to die for us. His death paid the penalty for our sins so that we don't have to pay the penalty ourselves. Jesus made it possible for us to be reunited with God and spend eternity in heaven with him after we die. But, Kristen"—Brad's eyes fixed on mine—"you have to personally choose to put your trust in Jesus and accept his forgiveness. Only then can you know for sure that you will go to heaven when you die."

I listened intently and nodded. Even though I didn't understand everything he said, I knew what he was saying was truer than anything I'd ever heard before. But even then I wanted more than just his word.

"Can you show me where it says this? You know, in the Bible?"

During the next half hour, Brad patiently showed me verses in his Bible.

"Psalm 139:13 says, 'For you created my inmost being; you knit me together in my mother's womb.' And listen to Romans 3:23, 'For all have sinned and fall short of the glory of God.'

"Romans 6:23 says, 'For the wages of sin is death, but the gift of God is eternal life in Christ Jesus our Lord.' "

And then there was John 3:16. As Brad read it, I remembered learning it as a child. "For God so loved the world that he gave his one and only Son, that whoever believes in him shall not perish but have eternal life."

The more I listened to him, and the more he read from the Bible, the more I understood that simply believing in God and being a good person wouldn't get me into heaven. I needed to do something more. *I need to accept Christ, to believe in him.*

I listened as Brad continued. I could tell he didn't want to walk away until he knew I understood.

"Kristen, there are just two more verses I want to read. Ephesians 2:8 and 9 say, 'For it is by grace you have been saved, through faith—and this not from yourselves, it is the gift of God—not by works, so that no one can boast.' "

Again I nodded as I listened. The verse that stood out to me the most, however, was the last one Brad read.

"Jesus said in John 14:6, 'I am the way and the truth and the life. No one comes to the Father except through me.' "

As my conversation with Brad wrapped up, he asked me if I wanted to pray and ask Jesus to forgive me of my sins and come into my heart and life.

Even though something inside wanted that, I shook my head no.

It wasn't the message I was rejecting. I was just shy. Most of the prayers I'd prayed before were recited ones I'd prayed at church or meals.

I also needed time to process. I always had a strong belief that there was a God, and I believed that Jesus was his Son. But mostly, I only knew *about* him. Before this night, I didn't know that he created me to be in a personal relationship with him or that there was a decision I had to make.

Yet what Brad said made sense. Before our conversation, I had always felt that God was far away and distant, and I didn't like that. It never felt right. I also knew that I was a sinner. After Brad and Val left, my parents cleaned up the house, and I continued to think about everything the Bible says. If sin did separate me from God and there was a price to pay for it, then there was nothing I could ever do that would make me good enough to get into heaven. Jesus' dying in my place seemed like a dream come true.

I also realized that if I had died the night I attempted suicide, I would have gone to hell, not because I'd killed myself, but because I hadn't accepted Christ as my personal Savior. It was a sobering thought.

But I didn't die. God kept me here, and I had another chance to accept Christ and know that I would spend eternity in heaven with God when I died. After coming so close to death and hell, I didn't want to put this decision off. I moved from my wheelchair onto the floor in my parents' dining room. I couldn't kneel, but I felt humbled to be in that position. I had a strange feeling God was meeting me on the floor.

I prayed, half with my mouth and half in my mind, "God, I need you to forgive me for my sins."

I know I can only be forgiven because of your Son, Jesus.

"I am so sorry I tried to take my life."

I know now that it wasn't mine to take.

"Please come into my heart, my life, and make it all better.

I can't do it. You're my only hope.

"I love you, God. Amen."

As I lay in bed that night, I felt good. I felt I had made the right decision. And God was proud of me. My body and my heart felt lighter, as if a huge weight had been lifted from my shoulders. And there was something more. A softness in the center of my chest that I could only describe as peace.

I turned to my side and snuggled against my pillow. I knew that my problems would still be there when I woke the next morning, but my most important question had been answered. *If I die I* will *go to heaven. Thank you, God, for a second chance.*

If you feel God tugging on your heart and you're ready to accept Jesus into your life and become a Christian...here is a simple prayer to guide you:

Dear God,

I want to become a true Christian. I confess that I have not lived a *perfect life.* I have sinned by living for myself and not for you. I have also failed to love you and obey you.

I realize that no amount of good behavior will ever erase all that I've done wrong. My only hope is in your grace and forgiveness. I know that Jesus died on the cross to pay the penalty for my sin.

I want Jesus to be my Savior (the forgiver of my sin) and my Lord (the leader of my life). I'm ready to live my life his way, with his help and strength.

Thank you God for forgiving me and making me your child. I can't wait to live a new life on earth and then to spend eternity in heaven with you.

Amen

If you just accepted Christ, your heavenly Father is overjoyed right now because he has been pursuing you for years! This is what he has been waiting for. You have a fresh start now. Don't let anything hold you back.

Remember, God wants you to talk to him, and he wants to guide you and help you through your life. You also need to learn how to listen to him and follow Jesus. Start going to a Bible-believing church in your area. You will learn and grow a lot there. You aren't meant to live the Christian life alone. Seek God with all your heart, and live to please him above all else. He will use you to do great things. I believe in you. You can do all things through Jesus.

In his love, Kristen

15

Trying to Remember

I climbed out of the car and wheeled into the counselor's office, unsure of what to expect. Despite the fact that this counseling practice had been recommended by the doctor who discharged me from the psych ward, I was wary.

I followed my mom into the large waiting room, replaying the details she'd told me. *The counselor's name is Ruth Ann. She was picked for me because she's the youngest, a single woman.*

I sat anxiously as my mom checked me in. *Here we go again.*

"Kristen Anderson." A woman with curly, short brown hair appeared in an open doorway. She smiled at me.

I smiled back, wheeling slowly toward her.

"Hello, Kristen. My name is Ruth Ann. It's nice to meet you. If you would, please, follow me. My office is down the hall."

We made our way down the long hall in silence, then turned into her office. Sitting at her desk, Ruth Ann looked down at her papers, then up at me.

"So, Kristen. Have you been in counseling before?"

"Yes. Once before. About a year ago."

"And what were your thoughts about it?"

"Well..." I paused, unsure how to answer. "The last counselor I had told my parents everything I said."

A look of surprise crossed her face. "You don't have to worry about that here. To break that trust would be completely unprofessional and against the law. Unless you are going to hurt yourself, or someone else, I will never tell anyone what you say."

Maybe she is different.

Over the following months, I came to trust Ruth Ann. I admired her integrity and professionalism...and her faith.

"I don't understand why I can't remember what happened," I said during one of our conversations. My stomach knotted. "I remember being at the park, and then the next thing I remember, my legs were gone, and I was lying by the side of the railroad tracks."

"Not being able to remember is normal, Kristen. Many people who go through traumatic events have said the same thing. It's possible you might never remember."

I thought about that for a minute. "I guess that makes sense, but I need to remember. I need to know what happened."

Ruth Ann offered a soft smile. "Don't worry, Kristen, you'll remember when you're ready. God protects us like that. He doesn't give us more than we can handle at a time."

Wow, I've never thought about it like that before. God actually does that?

I nodded. "Yeah, you're probably right."

"Have you ever prayed about it?"

"No." Since I hadn't been a Christian for long, I didn't really know what sort of things to pray for.

"Do you think it would help?" Ruth Ann asked.

"I don't know… I can try."

I sat on an exam table, my stomach a jumble of nerves. It was my first evaluation with the doctors and therapists at the Shriners Hospitals for Children in Chicago. We'd heard that this hospital was one of the top orthopedic hospitals in the country, and in order for me to be a patient in the hospital, I had to go through an application process. If I was accepted, I'd receive additional surgeries, prosthetics, and physical therapy.

"Would you tell us about your injuries, Kristen? How did you lose your legs?" one of the doctors asked.

My heart skipped a beat. Would the way I lost them limit my chances of being accepted?

What should I say? How should I answer? I bit my lip and looked down at the floor. *How can I tell him what happened when I can't remember everything?*

I looked to my mom.

"On January second, my daughter was run over by a train close to our home."

Her answer was simple. The doctor nodded, seeming satisfied.

Although the application process usually took six weeks, my mom received a phone call three days later from Shriners saying they wanted me to walk again. They'd accepted me as a patient. With their help, my rehab care would be free. My mom was thrilled. She told me that I'd be meeting with a prosthetist who worked with Shriners, and that he'd start building my prosthetic legs the following week.

The week went by quickly, and hearing about my upcoming graduation and my decision to participate in the ceremony, the prosthetist made it his goal to have my prosthetics ready so I could walk for graduation. After working with him for two weeks, it was finally time for me to go back to the Shriners hospital and try them on.

Excited, I wheeled myself down the colorfully painted halls to the examination room. My mom and brother walked beside me. A smiling nurse led me into the room. "Today's the big day, Kristen," she chirped.

My mom's hand moved to my shoulder and gave me a reassuring squeeze. I could sense her excitement, and deep down I hoped this day would be the day everything changed for the better. There was hardly a moment that went by when I didn't think about walking again. Sometimes I lay in bed at night and imagined what it would be like.

The orthopedic surgeon and physical therapist I'd been assigned were in the room with the prosthetist. My mom and brother sat on chairs, watching. From the looks on their faces, it was almost as if they took in hope with every breath.

"Okay, Kristen, we're going to take you through this step by step. First, you're going to put on the liners." He slipped one of the liners onto my leg, showing me how it fit, and then he took it off again. "Now it's your turn."

I rolled the silicon liners onto my residual limbs—one on each side. It reminded me of the way people put on pantyhose, but it wasn't as glamorous.

"See these pins here." The prosthetist pointed to metal pins at the end of the liner. "When you put your legs into the prosthetic legs, the pins will lock them in place. Next we'll fasten on what we call a corset," he continued. "It'll wrap around your thigh, above where the prosthetic leg will go. The corset will help stabilize your leg."

I watched as he locked the pin from the liner on my right leg into the socket of the prosthetic and slipped the corset around my thigh.

"Since your right leg still has its knee, it will have the most control." He laced up the corset and tightened it. Needles of pain shot up my leg, and I winced. It wasn't completely healed since the last surgery.

"You doing okay?" He paused and looked at me.

I glanced at my mom. Concern mixed with joy on her face.

"Yeah, I'm fine."

The prosthetist tied the laces. "Okay, your right leg is ready. Now I'll need you to stand up."

The nurse helped me to stand while the prosthetist put the left leg in position. I slid my leg inside it and then pressed down to lock in the pin. It reminded me of putting on sports equipment when I used to play soccer and hockey.

The nurse set the walker in front of me, and I grabbed it. The prosthetic legs felt heavy and uncomfortable. I stood, trying to balance, trying to ignore the sharp pain that radiated upward. I felt hot all over but focused on standing.

"Okay, Kristen, now we're going to try walking. You have a safety knee, which means you can only stand on it when it's in a straight, locked position.

This means you'll need to step, lock your knee, and then transfer your weight before you take another step."

My hands gripped the bars of the walker, and I swung my left thigh forward, making the prosthetic leg swing. Once the left heel hit the ground, I pushed the leg backward to lock the knee.

"Can you take another step, Kristen?"

I nodded, then I transferred my weight and moved my right leg. I clung more tightly to my walker, wishing I didn't feel so wobbly. Balancing was difficult, and it was very hard to walk—as if I were trying to walk on stilts. From a standing position, the legs looked like metal poles with feet.

I glanced at my mom and my brother. Tears of happiness filled my mom's eyes as she watched me. Ryan smiled from ear to ear.

The prosthetist looked at me. "They'll look much more real and lifelike once we get the covers on. Those will be done this week."

Pain caused my arms, legs, and body to tremble. "Will they always hurt like this? Will it always be this hard?" I asked the doctor.

"No, it will get easier, and you should get used to the pain. You'll do great."

I sighed with relief. "Good."

I can't wait.

I rode in the passenger's seat, enjoying the sunshine. Warm air streamed through the open window, blowing through my hair. It was a few days before graduation, and my mom was driving me back from the mall. We'd been shopping for an outfit for the graduation ceremony. As she drove she sang along with the music on the radio. Nothing seemed out of the ordinary until we approached the railroad tracks. As the front tires of the car touched the rails, I no longer saw the world outside the car. Disjointed images flashed through my mind.

I was on the swing, in the cold.

I was under the train, looking at my legs.

I was on the ground, the paramedics surrounding me, working on me.

I was sobbing like a small child beside the tracks.

Horror filled my chest. I felt like I was reliving that night again. I was there.

How did I get from the swing to the tracks? How did I get under the train? Could I have done this to myself? The thought filled me with disgust. Although I was beginning to suspect I had attempted suicide, I just couldn't be sure. There was an empty hole where the memory of those events should have been. *God, please help me remember.*

It was as if my mind had placed me in the middle of a scary, horrible movie, but it was my real life. My fists clenched in my lap. Overwhelming pain shot through me, the same pain I'd felt that night. I sucked in a breath, closed my eyes, and grabbed the armrest.

The images were there, and then they were gone.

I opened my eyes. The scenes had been so vivid I almost wondered if my mom had seen them too.

Even as I saw the familiar streets outside the window, my emotions were stuck in the memories, in the past, in the thoughts that were tied to those memories. It was hard to focus on the present.

My heart pounded as another surge of pain rushed through my body. Holding my breath, I fought to push down the thoughts. The harder I tried, the harder the memories pushed back.

I hated that I was reliving the scenes of the accident. This had happened a dozen times before. Each time it happened, the images grew clearer.

I didn't want anyone to know that I saw the images. I didn't want to talk about it.

I didn't know *how* to talk about it.

Why do I keep having these memories?

Can't I make this stop?

I just want to remember how I got on the tracks.

Life

16

One Step at a Time

The sun streaming through my bedroom windows promised a bright day, but inside my emotions felt anything but bright.

I can't believe today is graduation. I can't believe I'll be wearing my new legs there. I can't believe this is really my life.

The thoughts swirled around in my head. Too many thoughts. Too many worries. I pushed them to the side as I focused on getting ready. Once I was done with my hair and makeup, it was time to put my prosthetics on. I lifted my skirt and followed all the steps I was taught. Once they were on, I grabbed my walker and stood. Pain shot up my legs.

It's going to be okay. I can ignore it. They said I'll get used to it. Just walk.

I put one foot in front of the other and eventually made it to the full-length mirror on the front of my closet door. I had wondered what it would feel like to walk again. What I would look like once I had skinlike covers on the prosthetics.

When I looked into the mirror, my heart broke into a million pieces. I tried to hold in my emotions, but I couldn't. Tears streamed down my face. The picture I saw in the mirror didn't match what I'd imagined. Not in the least. My worst fears were coming true.

Things will never be like they used to be. It'll never be the same as having my real legs. Why don't they look like the ones that girl on Oprah *had?*

I hated everything about them. Still, I knew everyone wanted to see me walking. I sucked in a deep breath and wiped the tears off my face.

After grabbing my walker, I slowly made my way into the living room. My family stopped talking as I entered, and joy radiated from their faces. I smiled at them, then turned my focus back to walking. Each step came slowly as I looked down, making sure I knew exactly where my feet were going. I had to focus on my stride and not step too far or too close. With every step I cringed at the pain.

Part of me felt good. I enjoyed seeing my family's smiles, their excitement. For so long, it seemed—even before that night—I'd only caused them pain and heartache. Now I'd given them something to smile about, to hope for. I only wished what I felt inside matched the excitement I tried to show on my face.

The plan for the graduation was for me to sit in my wheelchair until my name was called. Then two of the teachers would come to me, and I would wrap my arms around them. They would help me walk to the front, get my diploma, and sit back down. It sounded like it would work, but I wasn't sure. I'd never walked that way before, and now I'd be doing it with everyone watching me.

What will everyone think? Will I be able to stay on my legs without falling? God, please help me.

On some level I wanted to show people that I was okay. I didn't want my friends, my classmates, or others in town to worry about me or feel bad for me. I wanted everyone to treat me the way they did before I lost my legs.

When we arrived at the school, my parents followed as I wheeled myself into the gym. All the chairs for the graduating students were on the gym floor. Students sat in them, facing the stage. Bleachers on the side were filled with parents, family members, and friends.

Since my last name was Anderson, I sat near the front and waited anxiously as the ceremony began.

I can't believe I'm at graduation in a wheelchair. I shouldn't even be here, shouldn't even be alive. I had never imagined my graduation would be like this.

After the usual speeches and introductions, a classmate stepped onto the stage. With little introduction, he launched into a parody of a popular song. He'd changed the words to reflect on our high school years and look toward the future. It was so hilarious that I almost forgot I was in a wheelchair. After a burst of applause, he left the stage, and the principal began to call the students to the stage to receive their diplomas.

"Kristen Anderson."

The dean and one of the gym coaches held my arms and helped me stand. My heart pounded as pain shot up my legs.

Please, God. Don't let me fall.

I placed my arms around their shoulders and took awkward steps toward a set of stairs. Since I couldn't climb the stairs, the principal walked down and presented me with my diploma.

Cheers erupted all around me. I sucked in a breath, and I smiled, pushing down the pain as I walked back to my wheelchair and sat. *I'm so glad I didn't fall.*

After the ceremony, many people came over to talk to me.

"It's so good to see you, Kristen."

"We're happy you're okay."

"It was good to see you walking on prosthetics."

"Thank you. Thank you for coming. It's good to see you too," I said at least a hundred times.

I tried to act as if I was okay. I tried to be happy about having prosthetics to use. I tried not to think about how much pain I was in, or how much I didn't like my new legs. I tried to focus on where I would go from here. And I tried to smile. Though none of my acting and smiling helped me feel better, I hoped it would help everyone else.

A month after graduation, I checked into Shriners for physical therapy. I was finally going to get used to my new legs and really learn to walk. My mom and dad walked beside me as I wheeled myself through the halls, glancing into the hospital rooms as we passed. I saw mostly small children. Some were in beds, others in wheelchairs.

Tension built in my chest the closer we got to my room. Everyone else was there because something had happened to them. But according to the police report, I'd done this to myself. What if it was true?

I watched a toddler in a tiny blue wheelchair wheeling down the hall. She laughed and smiled, and I was amazed and humbled by her attitude. As I watched her, I knew I'd been given a gift she'd never get—seventeen years with working legs.

I've experienced what many of these children have never had. A whole body. A healthy body. It was something I'd taken for granted. I wouldn't be able to do all the things I'd done before, but at least I had been able to experience them. *And now I'll be walking on prosthetics. I'll never take walking for granted again.*

As I wheeled into my room, I noticed I had a roommate, a girl who looked about my age. She wore some type of metal contraption connected to her head. It seemed to be holding her head in place. Her eyes met mine, and she offered a smile.

"Hi there. I'm Allison," the girl said. She had blond hair and blue eyes. Much of her hair had been shaved off, but what remained was very long.

"Hi, I'm Kristen." I smiled back.

I soon learned that Allie, as everyone called her, had recently become paralyzed in a horrible car accident. Her younger sister had also been injured.

"Our car was hit by a drunk driver," she told me. "It rolled down an embankment and landed on its roof." Allie spoke matter-of-factly.

A knot tightened in my stomach, and I pictured what that would have been like. *Oh my gosh, I can't imagine.*

"I'm so sorry." *I'm so lucky I've only lost my legs.*

"It's okay. Things are hard, but it doesn't help to get upset."

"Yeah...I suppose. Have you been here long—you know, at Shriners?" I dared to ask.

"Not too long. A few weeks. My mom and sister are here with me. We've heard good things about the rehab available for patients with spinal-cord injuries."

I listened, hoping Allie wouldn't ask me about my accident.

"Are you here for rehab too?" she asked.

"Yes, I'm, uh, going to learn to walk with prosthetics."

I felt bad even mentioning that someday I'd be able to walk again. Because of her injuries, Allie could hardly move, let alone get out of bed.

"What about you? Are you going to be okay?" I asked.

"I believe God works everything together for the good of those who love him."

It amazed me, really, to see how Allie's faith in Christ affected her attitude about life and what had happened to her. Having been a Christian for just four months, I hoped that someday I could have faith like Allie's.

"You know, it's been hard," Allie told me, "but I've forgiven the drunk driver. God has done so much for us, how can we not forgive?"

Her words stuck in my heart.

I wonder who I need to forgive?

Life

17

Conviction and Choice

My heart was heavy as Kevin and I drove back from the movie.

Nearly two years had passed since I lost my legs, and I was happy about the independence I'd gained. I drove my own car, held a job, and had even taken some classes at the community college. I lived in an apartment and had learned to maneuver through life in my wheelchair.

Kevin and I had been dating for about nine months. We talked about everything, hung out often, and became very close. Anytime I encountered an obstacle in my wheelchair and said, "I can't do that," he would help me figure out a way that I could. He didn't mind that I didn't have my legs, but it was still an issue for me, especially since I was unable to walk on the prosthetics I had. They were still too heavy and painful.

Since he lived closer to the theater, I'd picked him up that evening. After the movie, we sat in the car in his driveway and talked as we usually did. One hour passed, then two. Finally, Kevin told me he needed to go inside. He reached over to give me a hug good night. I held on, not wanting to let go.

I'd had more flashbacks that week. Even though they'd happened many times during the years since the accident, things were different now. This time, when the vivid movie played, I saw the train coming toward me. I saw myself lying down on the tracks.

I no longer questioned what had happened. Now I knew. *I did it. I did this to myself.*

"I have to tell you something...," I whispered into his ear. I hadn't planned on telling him, but the tension in my shoulders wouldn't ease.

Kevin sat back and studied my face. "What? Is everything okay?"

I bit my lip. I didn't know how to say it. Leaning back in the seat, I looked at him, then looked down.

"I think I laid down on the tracks." My words hung in the air. "I know that before I told you I wasn't sure...but I saw it. I remembered."

"Really?" he asked.

I couldn't speak. My shoulders shook as the tears came.

He stretched his arms to me, then pulled me into a hug, holding me against him.

"It's okay. It doesn't matter, Kristen. I'm just glad you're here. You don't need to worry about it anymore." His words were soothing, calming.

Kevin didn't say anything else; he didn't need to.

Over the next few days, I had a harder time adjusting to the truth. More questions trailed behind me, begging for an answer.

How could that be? How could I have done that?

For so long I had wanted to know how I got onto the tracks, but I hadn't wanted to be the kind of person who'd attempted suicide. I considered the act weak, cowardly, and selfish. I hated the pain and heartache my friends and family had faced. Now I knew the truth.

I did it. It was *my* fault.

It was nearly New Year's, but I wasn't celebrating. Knowing that I had actually attempted suicide filled my heart with pain, and a deep shame wrapped around me like a rusty chain. Familiar issues still plagued me—life without legs, the emotional struggle of depression, the fact I was on antidepressants, and the physical pain of my legs. On top of that, Kevin and I were having problems.

Ruth Ann had told me that I should check myself into the hospital anytime I thought I might hurt myself. I knew this was one of those times. I didn't want to, but I was having suicidal thoughts. When the struggle in my heart told me I wasn't safe, I followed Ruth Ann's advice.

While I was in the psych ward, I met a man in his forties and talked to him often. Not long before I met him, he had everything he ever wanted. He managed a company and had a wife and two kids. Then his wife left him, taking their two kids with her. His world seemed to crumble, and he didn't know what the point of his life was anymore.

My heart ached when I heard his story.

How can I help this man?

I took a deep breath, then spoke from my heart. "Two years ago, when I was in the hospital, I got a magnet with a Bible verse on it. It didn't mean much to me at the time, but now… Sometimes I feel like it's all that keeps me going. It says, 'For I know the plans I have for you,' declares the LORD, 'plans to prosper you and not to harm you, plans to give you hope and a future.'

"It helps me so much to know that even when I don't have plans for myself, I can trust that God has plans for me. Even when I don't have hope, he has hope for me. And even when I don't see a future for myself, he does. I just have to have faith.

"I know he has plans for you too."

As I spoke, his face brightened. He seemed to understand what I meant and to appreciate that I'd taken the time to talk with him. My heart smiled.

Maybe I can *help people.*

New Year's came and went. A few days later, I checked myself out of the psych ward, feeling better than I had in some time. I was still struggling, but reaching out to other patients had filled me with a renewed passion for life.

Maybe I *can make a difference.*

I let out a deep sigh. It had been nearly three years since I attempted suicide, and I sat in my apartment, looking at the hospital bed that had confined me for almost eight months as I recovered from another surgery.

I hope it was worth it.

The doctors had told me that this latest surgery would lengthen my femur, which would help me walk better with prosthetics. The surgeon broke my bone and then attached it to bars that penetrated through my leg and stuck out of my skin. Connected to the bars was a small key that had to be turned a quarter of a turn four times a day. As the key was turned, the bars pulled the pieces of bone farther apart, separating them so the femur could heal longer than it had been before. A longer bone was supposed to mean more stability and control for my prosthetic legs.

I chose to do the surgery, but I had underestimated the amount of pain I would face, and the doctors had underestimated the amount of time it would take to heal.

Hopefully my bone grew enough to help me walk better.

Since I wasn't walking yet, I couldn't be sure. The best thing that came out of those eight months was the way my dependence on God increased.

God, I need you, I would pray as my fists clenched with pain. *Please help me…help me deal with this pain.* My words were few, but I was confident that God could hear my heart. Minute by minute I could feel him answering my prayers and helping me through each day. I knew that I was never alone and that I would never have made it through such a difficult time without him.

In the end doctors remained undecided about whether the surgery would help me, but deep in my heart I knew that those months hadn't been wasted. If anything, the time helped me turn to God more. When I needed him, he was there. I learned that even through the pain I was not alone.

The next time I met with Ruth Ann, we talked about how things were going—how I was healing from my latest surgery and some of the challenges I was having.

"So how are you dealing with all of this emotionally?"

"It's hard."

"What's the hardest part?" Ruth Ann's face displayed concern.

"It's just, sometimes, I feel like less of a person without my legs. I don't feel whole."

"Do you think Jesus sees you as any less of a person, Kristen?"

What? I didn't expect that question. It took me a minute to think about it.

"Well, no. I guess not, but I still feel that way."

"Kristen, as long as you have Jesus in your life, you're not missing anything. You are a whole person in Christ. Try to follow him instead of your feelings.

"Remember how we've been talking about how you need to take responsibility for what you did. You realize there's no one else you can blame, right?"

"Yes, I know that..."

"But you have to forgive yourself too."

"Forgive myself—how?"

"Well, the day that you asked Jesus to be Lord of your life and forgive you of your sins, all of your sin—past, present, and future—was forgiven, right?"

I hesitated. "Yeah..."

"Well, if you continue to punish or condemn yourself, it's like saying that Jesus' payment for your sin wasn't good enough. I want you to memorize Romans 8:1." Ruth Ann jotted it down on a note card and handed it to me.

I read it out loud, "There is now no condemnation for those who are in Christ Jesus."

I placed the note card on the dash in my car so I could read it as I drove home. I repeated it over and over again, wishing I could believe those words deep down where it mattered most.

There was just a hint of cool air as I wheeled myself to my car after my Tuesday night class. When spring arrived in Illinois, new hope budded too.

Even though my body still faced daily pain, I was tired of my life being on hold. I didn't want to be held back from anything that others my age were doing. I wanted to prepare for the future.

"Kristen?" A woman's voice came from behind me. I stopped and turned.

I glanced up and saw a pretty woman who looked to be in her thirties. I'd seen her around campus before, but we weren't in any classes together.

"Yeah?" She seemed nice. I wondered what she wanted.

"Sorry to approach you like this, but I work with Kevin. He told me a lot about you, and I've seen you around campus, so I just wanted to say hi...and introduce myself. I'm Becky."

I liked Becky immediately. Something about her drew me in.

"I just wanted to encourage you," Becky said, as she told me her story. She had struggled through an abusive relationship, and her daughter had a congenital disease. Though the details were different, I could relate in many ways to the hardship she had faced. I could almost feel her pain. Then her story changed.

"A friend told me about a church nearby, so I decided to give it a try. I wasn't sure what to expect, but it was as if God met me there, in the middle of my pain. I could feel his love and acceptance. I have more strength and joy now that I have a relationship with Christ. I've gotten to know him better, and things aren't as hard as they were before. It's not like my situation's changed that much, but I'm able to go to God, and he helps me through it all. Before that day, I never knew I could know him like this."

Becky smiled. "I'm a single mom going back to school. It's hard, but God has done so many amazing things. I love him so much." Her face radiated peace and joy. After a while Becky glanced at her watch. "I can't believe we've been talking this long. I'm so sorry. I need to let you go."

"No, it's okay, really." I smiled. "I enjoyed talking to you. It's been good."

I looked at the clock in my car as I drove away, surprised to see that we'd been talking for *two hours.* I couldn't remember everything Becky said, but one thing stuck with me—this woman shined.

It was obvious to me that her relationship with God was the reason she had so much joy. In a strange way it felt right that I'd met her and she'd shared so much. Maybe it happened for a special reason. Maybe God had wanted me to meet her and experience that cool, special moment.

Seeing how Becky related with God triggered a longing I'd never felt before. As I got ready for bed that night, my mind was flooded with thoughts.

I accepted Jesus into my heart, into my life. I made a decision for him and became a Christian right after my accident. Why don't I know him the way Becky knows him? Why don't I have that kind of peace, joy, or love for life?

I knew that, in order for me to have a relationship with anyone, I had to talk to the person. The thing was, I didn't talk to God or pray very much. I usually talked to my friends, my family, or Ruth Ann about my life.

If God is as big and loving as he says he is, then he's even more concerned about the details of my life than my friends and family are. He loves me and cares about me more than anyone else. He must want me to talk to him about everything instead of going to everyone else first.

And since he's God, he has to have more answers. The right answers. Maybe he wants me to pray more often than just when I'm desperate, in pain, or in the right mood. I think that's the sort of relationship with God that Brad was saying we're all created for.

But how could I remember to talk to God that much?

God, I want to know you the way Becky knows you. What do you want me to do?

As I prayed, I felt that I needed to let God be my best friend, I needed to talk to him about everything, and I needed to listen to him and make him a priority.

Over the next few weeks, I started practicing that. When problems came up, I talked to God about them. And the more I did, the more I felt him with me. When I felt depressed, I'd pray and my perspective would change. When I was worried, I'd pray and I'd feel more peace. The changes weren't big on the outside, but I could feel them on the inside. And I felt God, too. The more I focused on him, the more I realized that having a better relationship with him was what I had always needed, longed for. Seeing how this one thing helped me made me want to change more.

I can do it... I am going to change my life. I was tired of living in the same old rut. I was ready to get myself back on my feet—if not physically, then emotionally. I was tired of fighting with depression. With God I could overcome it. I was sure of it.

18

I Can't Do This Alone

After showering and dressing, I reached for my medication. Just a few days before, I'd broken up with Kevin, a decision I was convinced was right, but I felt horrible. I missed him, and now my future seemed like one big question mark.

As I held the small bottles in my hand, something caused me to pause. *I know I don't need these. I need more of God in my life. I don't want to take these anymore.* The thoughts played over in my mind.

I couldn't imagine taking antidepressants for the rest of my life. When I took them, I felt as if I experienced everything one step removed from the world. An invisible barrier cloaked me. I no longer believed the medication was going to help me get out of my depression. I didn't like its side effects—drowsiness, memory loss, shaky hands. I looked at the antidepressants in my hand once again.

They haven't worked yet, and I've been taking them for years.

I wanted to be free of them. I thought that, maybe, if I stopped taking them, I'd really be able to move forward in my life.

I was ready for big change.

I can just stop taking them. No one will know.

I considered talking to my doctors, but I was afraid they'd talk me out of it. They had said over and over again that I would need antidepressants for the rest of my life.

I just have to do this. I'm gonna quit, cold turkey. I can't take it anymore.

I put the antidepressant bottles back on the shelf. If I truly wanted to depend on God, then I needed to do this. Didn't I?

The first day I couldn't tell any difference. The depression didn't get any better, but it also wasn't any worse. This made me happy. There weren't any emotional highs or lows, as I had feared. I felt…normal. I felt stronger. My dependence on the antidepressants had always made me feel weak. I felt more in control of my life than I had in a long time.

The next day everything seemed the same as the day before. *Did the medications have any effect on me at all? Why was I even taking them?*

Later that day, my friend Merick called to invite me to a party at his house. Though I didn't enjoy parties as much anymore, I thought it would be good for me to hang out with some friends. To get my mind off Kevin.

Merick carried me inside, and I was greeted by loud music and friends with drinks in their hands.

"Hey, Kristen." My friend John approached and held out a colorful bottle. "Have you ever tried one of these? I think you'll like it."

"Thanks." I smiled and took a drink, hoping to relax and have some fun.

Deep inside I knew I shouldn't be drinking. My motives weren't good, and the doctor had warned me that my pain medication doubled the effects of alcohol, but that didn't stop me. As the night went on, I had three drinks, which had the effect of six drinks. Soon I felt nauseated and dizzy. My emotions began to spiral downward, and I knew I needed to go home.

Once home, I went straight to bed, but I tossed and turned. My heart raced. My head pounded. My eyes wouldn't stay closed. Anxious thoughts filled my mind.

Things would be better if I could just walk.

What if I never walk again?

I miss Kevin.

If I could walk, I would be happy.

I'm never going to be happy with anyone else.

My mind sprinted from big details to small ones. Everything seemed to be wrong in my life.

When the sun dawned the next morning, I was still awake.

What's wrong with me? After the long night, the idea of suicide once again invaded my thoughts.

My body felt hot, sweaty. I had a pounding headache, and my vision was blurred.

I've been trying to choose God, to make choices that please him. Why did I end up like this?

I just need sleep. I closed my eyes and turned over, snuggling down under my blankets, but sleep didn't come.

I'm a horrible person.

Things are never going to get better.

I'm never going to be happy.

For the rest of my life, I'm going to fail.

Hours passed, and I was still in bed. A knock sounded at the door of my apartment.

Merick had come over to check on me.

As I went to open the door, the room spun. I tried to focus on Merick's face but couldn't.

"Kristen, are you okay?"

"Yeah, but she said...and I want... But I can't...and I don't know how. Why?"

Confusion filled Merick's face. "I don't understand, Kristen. Lie down. I'll be right back."

When Merick returned, my dad was with him. My mom showed up a few minutes later.

Seeing the state I was in, my mom hurried to my side. "Oh sweetheart, what's wrong?" I opened my eyes and focused on her furrowed brow, her frantic eyes.

I tried to explain, but the words tumbled out as soon as I opened my mouth.

"Kristen, you're not making any sense."

"Mom, sorry. I don't know what's happening."

Everything was blurry until, finally, sleep overtook me. A few hours later, my mom gently shook my shoulder. "Ruth Ann wants to talk to you."

I took the phone from her hand.

"Kristen, have you been taking your medication?"

I tried to remember. "No, I can't do it. It won't let me. I don't want to..." I knew I still wasn't making sense, but I couldn't make my words obey.

I can't do this anymore.

I can't get it right.

Things are worse, again.

I just want it to be over…

"Kristen." I heard Ruth Ann's voice again.

"Huh?" I opened my eyes and attempted to focus on her voice.

"Have you had any suicidal thoughts?"

"Yes, I don't care anymore. It's all wrong. I hate my life. It's too hard…"

"I'm concerned about you, Kristen. I want you to go with your mom… to the hospital. Will you do that?"

"No."

"Will you please go, Kristen? They'll be able to help you feel better."

I didn't care enough to argue. "Fine, but I still can't take it anymore."

"Kristen, can you tell me why you went off your medication?" a new doctor asked.

I wanted to tell him that I'd done everything the doctors and counselors had asked me to and my life was still a mess.

"I don't like what the antidepressants do to me, and I don't think they're going to help me get out of my depression." The words flew out of my mouth. I seemed to be talking a mile a minute, but I didn't care.

The alcohol had induced withdrawal symptoms from the antidepressants, and I was still feeling the effects. My thoughts raced, the doctor was blurry, and I felt nauseated.

The doctor asked my mom some questions, and I tried to decide if I still wanted to fight.

I want to be here, but I don't want to be here.

I thought about all the things I'd done to get better. I'd taken the medications the professionals had asked me to. I trusted that they knew what was best for me. I went to family counseling and individual counseling. I did my best, and it helped some, but the depression still clung to me, refusing to release me from its grasp.

If the antidepressants were going to really help, they would have worked by now. I've tried taking all the different ones they asked me to, and I'm still not better. If doing everything they've asked hasn't worked, then there is no point to taking them.

"Kristen, I believe you're bipolar. We'll need to change your medication."

What? Where did that come from? This is not me. This is not how I normally am.

Anger stirred within me at the doctor's words. He'd been with me ten minutes, and he was putting a label on me. Giving me this diagnosis was the easiest thing for him to do. I felt like he was just picking a new problem so he could give me more medication.

I knew I wasn't bipolar, and if the doctor had really known me or taken the time to read my files, he would have realized that.

The problem is that I've tried to get off my medications myself, cold turkey. The problem is that I was drinking on top of that. The problem is that I haven't been controlling my emotions.

For the third year in a row, I was admitted into the psych ward, and shame and pain filled every part of me. *Is there no hope? Will I ever make it?* I believed God wanted me to make changes in my life, but I assumed those changes had to come from my own strength, my own determination. Maybe I was wrong.

I wheeled myself into the common area of the youth psych ward. The previous two times I'd been in the adult section. Everyone there was much older than I was, so I'd had a hard time relating to the struggles they faced. The doctor thought the youth ward would be a better fit. I hoped he was right. The group therapy included quite a few young girls, needy girls who were broken and in pain. They talked about cutting themselves and how they hated themselves and everyone around them. As I listened to their stories, I wanted to share the hope I'd found in Christ, yet I feared it would sound hollow. My life was a mess. I was locked up in the psych ward along with them.

I had convinced myself that going off my medication meant I was trusting God—that it was an act of faith. Instead, it was an act of independence. I had taken things into my own hands and determined to make myself better in *my* time.

I can't live like this anymore. Oh God, I need you.

Tears filled my eyes.

Please, help me learn how to live for you, Jesus.

In the quiet of my room, I thought about how I'd ended up here again.

I've been so dramatic, seeing everything as either best or worst, and my up-and-down emotions reflect that. I need to grow up and be more intentional about my life. I need to focus on God more and start doing things more his way.

One reason I struggled was that I didn't know the Bible very well, and I didn't hang around with people who used it to guide their lives.

I picked up a notebook and considered things that would help me get better. I asked God for wisdom, and then I began to write.

I need to get off my medications with my doctor's help.
I seriously need to work at walking.
I need to surround myself with friends who have dedicated their whole lives to God.
I need to go back to church.
I need to focus completely on God.

Aside from focusing more on God and doing things his way, walking would be another key. The surgeries had taken their toll, and the prosthetics hadn't improved much. They still didn't fit right. They were heavy, ugly, and painful. I'd almost given up on walking.

I'd brought my prosthetic legs to the hospital with me and decided to practice walking during my free time.

Might as well try. It will be a step, or steps, in the right direction.

I put on my Adidas shorts, which made it easy to put my limbs into the legs and strap them on. I slid on my arm crutches, stood, and then walked around the halls outside my room for a while. Pain shot through my legs. Tears filled my eyes again, but I felt better knowing that I'd practiced.

I returned to my wheelchair, and as I was taking off my prosthetic legs, a nurse's aide in white scrubs entered the room.

"You've got some nice legs there," she said. "How do you like them?" There was no pity in her voice, just curiosity.

I shrugged and decided to tell her the honest truth.

"They're okay. They're just not like my legs used to be." I didn't want to be negative, but I couldn't be enthusiastic either.

"Well, when God gives you lemons, then you've just got to make lemonade," she spouted with confidence.

We chatted for a few more minutes, and then she hustled off to her duties. After she left, her words stuck with me. It was the simplest thing, yet it made sense.

Is it possible to take all the heartache and challenges I've been through and let them work for the better?

It gave me hope for change. It also made me think about something Ruth Ann had told me a year prior. "You're a strong-willed person, Kristen. You can either let that work for you or against you."

If I really am strong willed, and if God made me that way, I want it to work for me, not against me. I need to stop letting life happen to me, and do things his way.

I looked over my list again. "Church, godly friends, good choices." I thought about the church I'd visited recently. *I think that's where I'm supposed to be. I have to follow God, or my relationship with him and my life will never change. I can't let myself end up here again. I have to start living my life God's way. It's my only hope.*

19

Here for a Reason

I entered the high school building where the church services were held, feeling alone and nervous but excited too. Earlier that week, I'd visited a small church gathering for people in their twenties, and I'd already met some nice people. As I found a place to sit in the gym, a man approached me. He looked to be in his early thirties with blond hair and blue eyes. He held the hand of a little girl who looked to be about four years old. She offered me a shy grin and then hid her brown eyes from my gaze, tucking her face behind her daddy's leg.

"Welcome to The Chapel. I'm Jeff, and this is my daughter, Jorah. It's good to have you here. Is this your first time?"

"I was here once before. And on Wednesday I went to Incite."

"Oh yeah? How did you like it?"

"I liked it a lot. Everyone was really nice. The music was pretty cool too."

We chatted for a few minutes, and then he glanced at his watch. "Oh, I hate to run, but I better get going. Can I ask your name?"

"Sure, my name's Kristen."

"It was very nice to meet you, Kristen. I hope to see you here again."

Jorah waved as they hurried away. I waved and smiled back.

The band began the service by playing Christian worship songs with the words projected on a screen. I liked the music and found it easy to sing along. As I sang with the other people in the room, I felt happier than I had in a very long time.

When it came time for the pastor to speak, I was surprised to see the man who'd just talked to me approach the podium. He was *Pastor* Jeff.

As I listened to him, warmth filled my chest. "The most powerful life-changing force in the world is the love of God. When you begin to feel God's burning affection for you, it will transform you! You'll never be the same again." I felt like God had placed him there to talk directly to me.

Over the following months, I went to The Chapel as much as possible. I joined a women's small group and began reading my Bible, talking to God, and listening to Christian radio more often. Soon I felt as though I was walking straight out of my depression and into the arms of God. I told anyone who would listen what I was learning at church. I talked to my mom, and she decided to go to church with me. I could tell from the brightness in her eyes that she was happy for me. But I saw something else too—caution. It was as if she was waiting for trouble to come, the way it always had before. I hoped that this time things would be different. This time I *felt* different.

Please, God, help me stay on this path.

"Guess what, Kristen,"—my mom's excited voice carried over the phone line—"a friend of mine knows someone who works for a prosthetist. She said his company is working on a new type of legs. They are supposed to be much better."

I wanted to believe that there were better prosthetics out there—some that wouldn't hurt as much and would allow me to walk without crutches or a walker—but I didn't want to get my hopes up. I remembered how crushed I had been when my first prosthetics didn't turn out as I had expected.

When the day came for the new prosthetist to visit me, I hoped for the best.

A smile filled my mom's face as she opened the front door.

"Hello, Mrs. Anderson," said a man who was nicely dressed in black pants and a white, button-up shirt. "I'm Ray McKinney."

"Thank you so much for coming."

"It's my pleasure." He smiled warmly when he spoke, reminding me of my dad. "And who is this beautiful young lady? You must be Kristen."

I looked up and smiled. "Yes, I'm Kristen."

Excitement shone from his face as he explained the differences between the new and old prosthetics.

"The sockets use a vacuum system, which means there are no pins at the end of the liners, and you wouldn't have to wear the corset. And the best part," he said, a big grin spreading across his face, "is that they are light-weight and will hurt much less."

Wow, really? This is what I've been waiting for.

"Kristen, I believe we could get you walking without the assistance of a walker, crutches, or a cane."

"Do you really think so?" My heart pounded as I glanced at my mom. The tears in her eyes indicated that she wanted to believe his words as much as I did.

"I really do," Ray said. "Here's my business card. Please give me a call if you have any questions. It was wonderful to meet you."

"Thank you," I said, as I followed him toward the door, "It was wonderful to meet you too." As he left, thoughts ran through my mind.

Could it really be possible for me to walk again on my own, without crutches or a walker?

Those legs sound great. I'm sure they are expensive. Maybe when I finish school and get a good job, I can save up for them.

After a moment, my mom called me to the window, pointing to Ray's car as he drove away. "Did you see his license plate?"

I glanced out the window.

LEGMKR

" 'It's not about you.' What a great first line. I think I read it a dozen times," I said, looking at my friend.

Stacia smiled as she took a sip of coffee.

I'd met Stacia at the young adult's group at The Chapel. She was on staff at church and had a contagious smile, and we'd become good friends. One day she mentioned a book titled *The Purpose Driven Life.* "Do you want to read through it with me? We could meet once a week and talk about it."

I've heard of that book.

"Sure, I'd love to do that." I was interested in doing anything that would help me learn more about God.

We met in a coffee shop to talk about what each of us had been learning.

"I didn't realize it until now, but I think that for the longest time I mostly focused on myself," I told her. "I thought I needed to do that in order to get out of my depression, but this book has helped me understand things so much differently. I can't believe how selfish I've been."

Stacia laughed. "Maybe that's all of us."

"Yeah, maybe... But you know, I think that was part of my depression. Everyone told me I had to take care of myself to get better, so I did. I wanted to get out of my depression more than anything, but focusing on myself was the wrong thing to do. God should have been my main focus...and he wasn't. It's no wonder I was stuck in a cycle of depression for so long. Selfishness doesn't bring happiness."

Stacia nodded. "No, that's for sure. But it's great to see how much better you're doing now, Kristen. You're growing in your relationship with God, and I can only imagine how he'll use you in the future."

Stacia and I talked more as the weeks passed, and our times together were always encouraging. I also began blocking out time every day to spend with God, read my Bible, and pray. One day as I sat in the comfy blue chair by my front window, I prayed that God would be real to me—as real as Stacia was when we were together.

Each day I spent that time with him, he filled me with more peace, joy, and understanding. My relationship with him was better than it had ever been.

"Many are the plans in a man's heart, but it is the LORD's purpose that prevails," I read in Proverbs 19:21. *My plan for years has been to walk, to get better, to be happy...but what are God's plans for me?*

I reread one of my new favorite passages: Ephesians 2:10. "For we are God's workmanship, created in Christ Jesus to do good works, which God prepared in advance for us to do."

God, what did you keep me here to do besides have a personal relationship with you? I love knowing you, but what "good works" have you prepared in advance for me? I considered my talents, my gifts, my passions.

The words *ministry* and *missions* stirred emotion inside my chest.

Really, God?

I took a deep breath and looked toward the ceiling.

Could God really choose someone ordinary—like me—to do his work?

I thought about my college social-work classes. I figured if I got a job being a social worker, I could help people find work, housing, and food. I'd also considered working with troubled teens.

Now I realized that instead of helping people with their physical needs, I could introduce them to Jesus. I could tell them about God.

That would help people more than anything. Just like it's helped me. Lord, is that what you want me to do?

As I prayed, I was filled with more peace, joy, and purpose than I'd ever had. It was as if God was giving me an answer to what I'd been trying to figure out since right after the accident when people told me, "There's something you're supposed to do here, Kristen."

During the following weeks, I continued to read my Bible and pray about what it would mean to serve God in full-time ministry. I figured it would be amazing, but I probably wouldn't make much money. I was okay with that. Money and material possessions had never brought the happiness I desired.

But if I go into ministry, I will probably never be able to afford the prosthetics Ray told me about. They're too expensive. Health insurance only pays for part of the cost.

God, I don't know what to do. I always thought you wanted me to walk.

As the days passed, my excitement grew about telling others about God through full-time ministry.

God, if you want me to walk again, you'll make it possible, I prayed. *I won't worry about that. For now I'm going to focus on knowing and serving you. Show me the next step.*

One of the radio stations I listened to regularly was affiliated with Moody Bible Institute in Chicago—basically in my backyard. I went on the Internet to find out more information about the school. The programs looked great, but the cost seemed prohibitive.

I'll never have enough money.

I've never been a great student.

I doubt they'll accept me.

I decided it wouldn't hurt to try, and I started by taking one online class. I also worked to save enough money to attend full time the next semester.

Show me your will, Lord. I want to follow you—even if it means I'll never walk again.

"Happy birthday, Kristen!" Dozens of voices rang out as soon as I entered the door. My new friends at The Chapel had thrown a birthday party for me. One of the girls, Michele, had organized everything, and the party was at her sister's house. I could hardly believe that all those people where there for me.

I tried not to wince in pain as I entered the house on my prosthetic legs. While I'd become comfortable with who I was in my wheelchair, walking was a dream I still held on to. My legs hadn't improved, but I was trying to use them more regularly. I felt like a toddler as I struggled to walk.

I can't believe I'm twenty-one and can hardly walk. I hope soon it will hurt less and I'll be able to walk more.

After the party, Michele's sister, Tammy, walked with me to my car. "I don't know if you realize this, Kristen, but my husband was on duty the night of your accident."

"Really?" I felt my jaw drop. "What? Are you serious? Wow…I didn't know."

Tammy crossed her arms over her chest. "Yeah, Bill was one of the paramedics. When he came home that night, I could tell that something had really shaken him up. He told us a seventeen-year-old girl had lain down in front of a freight train. He told us her legs had been cut off and that they didn't know if she would live. Our hearts went out to her—to you—and so we held hands right there in the kitchen and prayed."

They prayed for me? Wow.

"We didn't know anything about you, but our hearts were broken for you. We prayed that you'd survive and also that you'd find hope in Christ."

My throat tightened, and I swallowed hard. "Wow, you didn't even know me, and now I'm here. God seriously answers prayers."

"He does, Kristen. In so many ways. I have to admit that I was mad when yet another call took Bill away from the house, but that night I realized how important my husband's job is." Tammy smiled. "The first time we saw you at The Chapel, Bill leaned over to me and said, 'I think that's her. That's the girl.' He was so excited."

"Seriously?" I asked.

"Yes, Kristen, seriously."

As we talked, Bill walked outside toward us. I wasn't sure if I wanted to meet him—after all, he'd seen my brokenness and pain.

But as Bill got closer, thankfulness poured out of me. "Tammy just told me you were there that night. I can't believe it." I searched for words to try to express the depth of gratitude I felt, but nothing seemed to suffice. "Thank you for everything you did for me."

"You don't have to thank me, Kristen; it was my pleasure. You know, we didn't think you were going to make it. You lost about eight pints of blood. People are supposed to die after they lose five. When I first saw you, I was shocked you were still alive. I've seen people die from far less serious injuries. There's no doubt that God saved your life that night, because medically... well, medically your survival was impossible. And now look at you. You're standing, walking. I wouldn't have imagined that would ever happen."

"It was a miracle," Tammy said.

Bill nodded. "You don't know how big a miracle. Kristen, did anyone tell you they tried to bring in a Flight for Life helicopter for you, but it was too foggy?"

"No."

"Instead they did something I hadn't seen before and I haven't seen happen since. They radioed in and had all the intersections between where you were and the hospital blocked. A drive that normally would have taken forty-five minutes took only eight minutes. I think we were all so surprised you were alive that we wanted to make sure we did all we could."

Goose bumps rose on my arms, and my heart pounded in my chest.

"God kept you here for a reason, Kristen."

Life

20

Faith and Forgiveness

Ever since my last trip to the psych ward, I'd been waiting to talk to Ruth Ann about getting off my antidepressants—the right way. I knew I needed them right after my suicide attempt, but not anymore. The doctors had told me that because of my family's history, they believed I had a genetic chemical imbalance and would need to be on antidepressants the rest of my life. For three years I'd told myself, *Depression is a part of you. It's in your genes. You can't change it. Just deal with it.*

But the more I learned about God, the more I believed he didn't want me to be depressed. Many times Ruth Ann had told me, "You don't have to stay where you are, Kristen."

Over the past few months my life *had* changed. God had helped me quit smoking and drinking, and I believed he could help me live a good life without antidepressants.

I decided to talk to Ruth Ann about it. "My doctors told me I'd have to take antidepressants for the rest of my life."

"Yes, I know. I've read your files."

"Do you think I have a serious problem, like I'm bipolar or something?"

I focused my gaze on her.

"No, Kristen. Your history doesn't show that."

Her statement was simple, but with those words I felt lighter. "Besides," she continued, "you know yourself better than anyone else. Do you think it's time to start weaning yourself off the medication?"

"I really do. I've prayed about it a lot. Can you think of any reason that I need to stay on the medication?"

"I can't be sure, but you can always go back on antidepressants if you need to. I don't believe you have to be on them if you feel you can handle things without them."

"Yeah, that's how I feel. I have an appointment coming up with my psychiatrist. I was thinking I would talk to him about it then."

"That sounds like a good plan, Kristen."

I sat in the doctor's office, waiting for my appointment and thinking back to the last time I'd gone off my antidepressants. I hoped I was doing the right thing—what God wanted me to do—and not just what I wanted. I trusted that if God was leading me in this decision, everything would work out okay.

I was seeing the same psychiatrist who'd admitted me into the psych ward during my last visit. It was hard to believe that I'd been in there just three months prior. So much had changed.

"You're bipolar, Kristen. You need these drugs."

I ignored his glare. "I understand you think it's best I stay on them...that I need them. Thank you for your opinion, but I want to try getting off them. Will you help me?"

"How long are you talking about? How soon do you want to get off?"

"As soon as possible. Will you help me?" I repeated.

He sighed, "I will, but I really do not recommend this. You will be back on them before you know it."

"I'm sorry, but I don't agree. God has become a much bigger part of my life, and I think he will help me—"

"Well," he interrupted. "The soonest I recommend is sixty days. I'll give you a lower dosage every two weeks. We'll monitor you closely and see how you do."

My heart leapt as I clasped my hands on my lap.

"Okay, that sounds great."

I made two appointments to return, and I left the office with a lighter prescription than I'd had before.

Thank you, God. Thank you...

A few weeks later I began to feel more sensitive, more emotional. One night I was talking on the phone with a friend, and we had a small disagreement. While I tried to keep my voice calm, I felt my emotions building. It was as if a thin layer of ice was cracking around my heart. Ripples of pain, sadness, longing, and knowing mixed together, and the tears came.

My throat grew tight and thick. As a tear broke free, I realized I hadn't cried for a very long time.

While on the medication, I'd not only lost my emotions, I'd also lost some of my memories. People often talked about events or places I'd experienced, and for me it was as if those things had never happened. Sometimes I could remember only part of what they remembered. Other times I remembered nothing at all.

It was as if I'd been sleepwalking. Now that I was awake, I was able to feel much more and see my life more clearly.

One of the first things I realized was how much of my life revolved around my pain pills. Doctors had told me I would need them the rest of my life, and I'd gotten used to watching the clock to know when to take them. If I missed a dose, I knew it right away.

One day, while visiting the pain specialist, I told him I wanted to get off my pain meds.

"I don't think that's possible, Kristen. You faced major trauma. I've told you before, your body will always have chronic pain." He told me that while he couldn't force me to take them, he recommended that I keep the pills on hand, should the pain overwhelm me. I again asked for a plan to help me get off the medication, and he gave me lower doses, reminding me that it was okay to take more if needed.

I noticed the difference right away. As I expected, the pain was intense. The sharp pains came the way they usually did, but the lower-dosage medication wasn't enough to mask it. The muscle spasms were stronger, and phantom pains returned. Sometimes I'd cry from the sharp stabs of pain that shot up my legs. It would have been easy to take more pain medication, but I wanted to trust God in this area of my life too.

Every time I wanted physical relief, I'd pray. Knowing I couldn't face this alone, I asked people in my small group to pray with me, for me.

God, I need you. I want you to be my pain reliever. Please help me.

Time and time again I felt my prayers answered as the pain subsided. As the weeks passed, the pain lessened, and my tolerance grew along with my faith in God.

The sun was bright with just a hint of clouds as I arrived for another appointment with Ruth Ann. Sort of like my emotions. Sort of like my thoughts.

Ruth Ann leaned forward in her chair and smiled. "So, how have you been?"

"Many things have been better, actually, but it's weird. Since going off my antidepressants, I can really feel things in ways I haven't felt them before. I'm more emotional."

"That's understandable, Kristen."

"It's almost as if I'm just beginning to be really, really sad about losing my legs. I look at my pant legs, see that they're empty, and I feel horrible. I find myself wanting to buy shoes."

"Kristen, I think you need to let yourself be sad about your loss."

"What?" I furrowed my brow. "What do you mean? I just want to be happy. I don't want to be sad. I mean life is going so good..."

"There are times when it's okay to be sad or upset, Kristen. God gave us all types of emotions, and it's good for us to have them. It's good that you're not numb anymore. I think you'll finally have a chance to let go of it. All of it. It's been a heavy weight to bear, hasn't it?"

I nodded. During the next few days I read my Bible and prayed. Sometimes it was hard when the emotions came, but it was good to know that God hadn't given up on me and he never would. I knew as I continued to seek him, he would change me, help me.

Lord, help me. Take it all away—all the stuff that doesn't belong.

I imagined giving it to him—the sadness, the shame, and the guilt. I also thought of myself—the depressed person that I had been—and I forgave myself for my choices. My body would never be whole again, but my soul was, and I could see myself as God saw me.

Clean, forgiven, new.

21

Overwhelming Gratitude

I had been attending The Chapel for a few months when I heard there would be a meeting after church for anyone who was interested in being baptized.

"You don't need to be baptized to dedicate your life to Jesus. Instead it's proof to those around you that you've chosen to live for him," Brent said at a church meeting. "Going under the water is a symbol of dying to your old life, and coming out of the water is like rising into your new life with God."

I wasn't sure what my parents would think, since they had already had me baptized when I was an infant, but I wanted to do everything God wanted me to do.

I noticed the baptism would be held at a local lake, and I hesitated, knowing I wouldn't be able to roll into the water at the lake. I told Brent my concern, and without a second thought he said someone could carry me. I was happy he didn't seem to see it as an obstacle, and at the end of the meeting, I put my name on the sign-up sheet.

Afterward, in the quiet of my living room, I began writing my testimony. As I wrote, I suddenly realized I had a beautiful story to share. God had been working in so many of the details of my life through the years.

Lord, you never gave up on me. Never.

Gratitude filled my heart. I was grateful that I'd lost my legs. That, more than anything else, had brought me to Christ.

What if it had never happened? I shuddered, thinking of where I could be. Losing my legs showed me how big and real God is. For the first time I realized losing my legs was worth it. I wouldn't go back, even if I could.

For so long, I'd been focused on another romance—on relationships I had in this world—but the pain of breaking off those relationships pushed me into a deeper, more intimate relationship with God. I needed this. More than anything, I needed him.

Thank you, Jesus.

Tears came as I wrote down my story, God's story—our love story.

The day of my baptism was warm with a light breeze as we assembled at a private beach on Gages Lake. I wheeled slowly through the sand, looking around at the forty people who'd come to watch. My mom, dad, and brother, Ryan, were there, along with many of my new friends from church. After a few minutes, my name was called, and I wheeled myself to the microphone.

"Growing up, I always thought my family was much more religious than the other families I knew. We went to church every Sunday, I was baptized as a baby, and I had my first communion. I went through confirmation and all that—but by the time I was seventeen, I still didn't know Christ." I paused and struggled for breath as emotion flooded through me. "I knew *of* him, but I didn't know him in my heart as I do now.

"Before I started living for God, I lived for my family and for my friends and for many material things. I was not very obedient to God—and that was disastrous. But fortunately the disaster that ended that part of my life was exactly what God used to bring me closer to him.

"Most people assume that I lost my legs in an accident of some sort, but if you've ever asked me, you know the truth. For those of you who don't know me, I lost my legs because I attempted suicide"—my voice quivered—"when I was seventeen..."

I took a deep breath. "I laid down on train tracks. Um, I don't want anyone to feel bad or sorry for me, because God saved me that night, and since then he's put so many people into my life to bring me closer to him. It hasn't been easy—because I went through a bunch of operations and a lot of pain—but God was awesome. He put some strong people in my life who were very supportive and very encouraging. And he's been very gracious to fill my heart with forgiveness for trying to take my life that night. I'm so thankful to him for keeping me here and saving me that night because it is such an honor to serve him, and I can't wait to see how he uses me in the future."

When I finished, Pastor Jeff and Brent came over to me. I put an arm around each of them, and they lifted me from my wheelchair. When we got chest deep, they turned around so I was facing everyone.

I looked to Pastor Jeff, and he smiled.

"Kristen, have you come to a place in your life where you have committed to trust and follow Jesus Christ as your Lord and Savior?"

I smiled back, grateful and overwhelmed. "I have."

I leaned back as they lowered me into the water and then lifted me back up.

Humbled and wet, I exited the lake in Jeff's and Brent's arms. A smile filled my face because I knew I'd done something important—something that God wanted me to do.

My relationship with God was public knowledge now. Everyone knew I was living my life for him and him alone.

I sat with my family as fifteen others shared *their* stories and were baptized. As the service ended, Brent led everyone in a worship song.

When the song ended, he spoke into the microphone.

"If you're here today and you haven't made the decision to accept Christ's forgiveness, I'd like you to pray with me.

Everyone bowed their heads and closed their eyes. He said a simple prayer, and in my heart I prayed for those who might be making a decision for Christ that day.

"Now, if you've just made the decision to accept and follow Jesus Christ for the first time...would you raise your hand? We'd love to congratulate you and welcome you into God's family."

I saw movement to my right, and I turned my head. I watched with awe and joy as my mom raised her hand.

Thank you, God, for what you're doing in my family. Thank you for bringing all of us to this place.

Later that afternoon I talked to my mom about her decision.

"Mom, I'm so happy for you." I pulled her into a big hug. I noticed a smile on my dad's face and hugged him, too. God was working again, in new and different ways.

I wheeled into The Chapel's youth center on a Tuesday night, taking in the chatter of teens, the busyness of kids in motion, and the excitement that stirred in the air. Music and life filled the large room.

I wish I had known there was a place like this when I was still in high school.

For a long time I'd wanted to help teenagers, but now that I'd volunteered, doubts and insecurities flashed through my mind as I looked around the room.

I'm not that much older than they are. Why would they listen to me? God, you brought me here, but I feel so unqualified.

Amazingly, the teens not only listened to me but also embraced me. Week after week I shared my life with them—my mistakes and what God had taught me since that January night—and they opened up to me.

Soon I began leading a freshman girls' small group. Some of the girls were strong Christians; others were on the edge of their faith. Despite their differences, they all had one thing in common—in some way they all felt broken. And I could relate. I remembered the pressures of high school and could identify with the pain they felt. I did whatever I could to encourage them, but I knew they needed more. They needed Jesus, just as I had needed him.

One day the youth pastor asked me to share my story with the students. I was reluctant at first. The only time I'd told my full story was at my baptism, but I wanted these teens to know that God is real and that nothing compares to doing life with him.

Maybe they will learn from my mistakes. Maybe they won't wait until something horrible happens to them before they give their lives to Christ.

I started out talking about the things that had contributed to my depression and suicide attempt—the deaths, the rape, Brandon's suicide, the arguments with my parents. Then I talked about that night.

My voice shook as I told how God had saved my life, how he'd saved my soul, and how he'd transformed my heart and life into something I could never have imagined. Every eye was fixed on me as I spoke. The room was silent.

After I finished, many students crowded around to talk with me. My heart pounded. I had never expected such a response.

Several of the teens shared that they'd struggled with depression and had suicidal thoughts. Some had even attempted suicide. As I listened to their stories, I was humbled by the way they opened their hearts to me. But I felt burdened, too. I desperately wanted them all to know the difference Jesus could make in their lives.

I hadn't intended to become a speaker, but after that night, God helped me see that it was part of his plan. Soon I began receiving invitations to tell my story at other youth groups and churches. Everywhere I went, people were amazed at how God had saved me and turned my pain into peace and joy. Each time I spoke, I felt privileged that God had given me a story that showed his amazing faithfulness.

After the speaking events, people often e-mailed to thank me for sharing my story. Still others wanted me to be their friend, to hang out with them and give them encouragement and advice.

It soon became obvious that I couldn't connect with everyone who needed help. I had difficulty sleeping at night, knowing my inbox was filled with e-mails from people who needed help and hope. Often, as I lay in bed trying to sleep, I prayed, asking God for direction.

Lord, there are so many people who need the peace and joy I've found in you.

Please show me how I can best reach them. Continue to change me, guide me, so that I can better point the way to you.

"Something happened the night of my accident that I haven't told you about, mostly because I never knew what to think of it," I told Ruth Ann during one of our sessions. Lately, I'd been thinking about all the ways God had brought me closer to him...including that night on the tracks.

"Really, what is it?"

"Well, it was something that happened as I was lying on the side of the tracks after the train went over me. I thought I was dying and...well..."

Ruth Ann waited patiently as I tried to put together my thoughts.

"I remember crying for my mom, like a little kid would. Then I remember hearing the song 'Amazing Grace.' It wasn't like I heard it out loud, but in my heart and mind, I heard it really loud and clear. And at the same time, I felt a ton of peace—it was like nothing I'd ever felt before. Do you think that's really weird? Is that possible?"

Ruth Ann's smile lit up her face. "I think that's definitely possible, Kristen. I think God was trying to talk to you and touch your heart through that song. Like a message to you from him...amazing grace."

I went through the words in my head.

Amazing grace, how sweet the sound,
That saved a wretch like me.
I once was lost, but now am found.
Was blind, but now I see.

"I've thought that maybe he just wanted me to know that he was there with me, saving me."

"I'm sure you're right, Kristen."

"But also that he wasn't only going to save my life. I feel like he wanted me to see him in that song, like he was drawing me to himself so my soul could be saved too. I was getting a second chance that I didn't deserve...to live, to know him, and to go heaven."

Ruth Ann smiled.

"That really is amazing grace," I exclaimed.

I love that song now. I feel like it's my song...between me and God.

Amazing Grace...

Life

22

Ways I Never Imagined

Almost a year had passed since the last time I was in the psych ward. I still couldn't believe how much my life continued to change.

I prayed as I drove to my counseling session with Ruth Ann. *Thank you, God, for everything. I wouldn't be where I am or who I am today if it wasn't for you. I owe all that I am to you. I love you so much.*

There had been occasions in the past when I wanted to stop counseling. I didn't like the time it took or the cost. But I'd learned the hard way that my way didn't really work. Instead, I needed to follow God, wait on him, and in this case, trust Ruth Ann's judgment.

Our session went as usual. We talked about my life, work, college classes, church, my speaking, and mentoring younger girls. At the end of the hour,

I wrote Ruth Ann a check and then paused, waiting for her to schedule the next appointment. Instead, she looked at me and smiled.

"Kristen, I think you're doing really well. You've come a long way. I'm very pleased with your progress. I don't think you need to come anymore unless you think you need to."

"Really?" I smiled. It pleased me to know that Ruth Ann saw my positive changes.

"Yes, I really think so. What do you think?"

"Well, I think you're right. I've been doing really well. But I wanted to keep coming as long as you thought I needed to."

Ruth Ann beamed. "That's great, Kristen. The old you wouldn't have done that. Thank you."

"No, thank you. For everything." It felt as if a weight had been lifted off my chest. "So what now?"

"Well, you know my feelings on counseling. I don't think that this should be the last time you ever see a counselor, but I'll always be here if you want to talk."

"Okay," I nodded, still smiling. "Would it be all right if I gave you a hug?"

As she leaned down to hug me, the thought of not seeing Ruth Ann again brought mixed emotions. I knew it was right for me to move on, but I would miss her.

As I turned to leave, I saw another patient waiting just beyond the doorway. I glanced back at Ruth Ann one last time and said good-bye. Wheeling into the waiting room, I could hear the familiar words from behind me.

"Hello. My name is Ruth Ann. If you would, please, follow me. My office is down the hall." Our relationship had ended. Theirs had just begun.

I leaned over the sink, rinsed soap from my face, and wished the water could rinse away the tension I felt. It had been a good day but a long one. I'd worked until four thirty, then eaten a quick dinner before going to my small group. Since coming home, I'd completed an assignment for my theology class and tried to get through a few of the e-mails I'd received after speaking earlier that week. It was now twelve thirty, and I was exhausted.

I toweled off my face, then turned out the light.

I lay awake in my bed, my heart restless as I thought about the dozens of e-mails that waited in my inbox. E-mails from people who were hurting, lost, hopeless, and depressed. E-mails that waited for my response. I'd answered as many as I could, but I never felt like I was answering enough of them. I needed other people to help me, but how?

When I started attending Moody Bible Institute, I assumed most of my ministry work would wait until after I graduated. But as I lay there, thinking of all those people reaching out for help, I was no longer sure God wanted me to wait.

I felt that God wanted me to start an organization that would help me reach out to those people, wherever they were.

As I lay in bed, the name *Reaching You* popped into my mind.

Thank you, God. I couldn't have thought of anything that fit better.

In the months that followed, I asked my family, friends, and small group at church to pray as I took small steps to connect those who were hurting with those who could offer help.

Soon people began to volunteer time and resources, each indicating that they felt God leading them to help. Before long, we set up a Web site and e-mail accounts and started the official paperwork. Now, more than ever, I knew that God wanted me to continue in my ministry training, but I wondered how I could pay for the rest of my classes since I'd quit my job in order to run the ministry. I trusted God and began to pray.

God, thank you for the ways you have blessed this ministry. You know my concerns. You know the plans you have for my life. I don't know how it's all going to work out, but if you want me to serve you in this way, I trust that you will provide the resources to do so. Please show me how.

The answer to my prayers started with my parents a few months later. Since attending The Chapel, they'd become part of a small group, and one night my parents asked the members of their small group to start praying for the money I needed to finish Bible college. The group decided that they would not only pray, but they would also be part of the answer.

The next day, group members approached people in the community and set up a fund-raiser. Items flooded in for a silent auction as the group recruited more volunteers, created fliers, and planned food and decorations. Musicians signed up to help, and before long I was getting calls from newspaper reporters who wanted to know my story.

The night of the event felt like it could have been my wedding day. People from all parts of my life attended—people I knew growing up; people from work, school, and church; and many people I didn't know—all there to "Help Make A Difference" as the flier said, and donate their time and money out of their love for God and for me. I was overwhelmed with gratitude.

During the night, I tried to talk to and thank as many people as I could. Everyone voiced support.

Even my nephew Noah, who was five, approached me, pulling some coins out of his pocket. "This is all I have, Kristen...but I want you to have it."

Tears filled my eyes, and I hugged him tight.

"Thank you, Noah. To me and God, it's a lot."

I was scheduled to share my story in the middle of the event. As I looked around at my friends, family, and supporters, I realized my story was their story too.

At the end of the night, almost $18,000 had been donated. It was just the tuition I needed to finish my degree. I was excited but not surprised. I was learning every day that when I followed God, he would provide for all my needs.

All of them.

Having chosen ministry and Bible college over full-time work, I had given up hope of ever getting better prosthetics. For so long, walking had been my primary focus. I'd had numerous surgeries that the doctors said would help prepare my legs for prosthetics. For so long I'd evaluated my life based on whether or not I was walking. But as the months passed and I started helping other people, I discovered that doing God's will mattered even more than walking. Even though I still hoped that I'd walk again someday, reaching others and telling them about Jesus became more important.

One day during a regular prosthetic visit, Ray smiled broadly as he walked into the appointment room carrying my prosthetic legs. "Guess what, Kristen? I have something exciting to tell you."

"Really?" The joy on his face caused my heartbeat to quicken. "What is it?"

"You know my partner, John McDonough?"

"Yeah..."

"Well, John and some others got together and started a nonprofit organization for amputees who deserve state-of-the-art prosthetic limbs but cannot afford them. We're going to provide the best—for free." Ray grinned. "I was talking to him the other day, and we thought you could be the first recipient. We just need you to fill out this application."

I was speechless, humbled at his words. Ray and John had thought of me out of all the people who could use prosthetics.

"That's cool. So..." I glanced at the application and then back up at Ray. "What happens if I'm accepted?"

Ray shook his head and smiled. "Don't worry, Kristen, you will be accepted. Then I'll finish building your prosthetics. They'll be better than you can imagine, and whatever your insurance doesn't pay the organization will."

"Wow..." My mind spun, trying to take in everything he said. "Is there a catch?"

"Our goal is to get worthy people like you walking again. That's all."

"This is such a blessing, Ray. I can't believe it. Is there anything I can do to help?"

"Well, once your legs are done you can walk." He chuckled as he spoke. "That would really make us happy."

I bit my lip as reality sunk in. Even though I didn't know how I would pay for better prosthetics while I was in school, God was showing me that he could provide for me in ways I never imagined.

Wow, God. I'm doing what you've called me to do. And now you're making it possible for me to serve you and *have legs? I couldn't have dreamed of more. You are so amazing. Nothing compares to knowing you. Thank you, God, Thank you.*

I sat in my wheelchair at the back of the stage, waiting to be introduced. Lately, I'd not only been speaking in Illinois and Wisconsin—I had also been invited to travel and tell my story in other places: Texas, Mississippi, and New Jersey, to name a few.

My stomach quivered slightly—not from nervousness, but rather from excitement. I was getting more and more chances to share the hope I'd found in Christ with others, and many people were making decisions to accept and follow Jesus themselves. Reaching You Ministries was gaining more volunteers, prayer, and financial support too.

Finally, I heard someone announce my name. As I wheeled onto the stage, the lights were bright, and I felt a familiar nervousness. No matter how many times I'd done this, the first few moments were never easy. I took a breath and reminded myself that it was not just my story, but the story of God's work in my life.

"Good evening. Thank you so much for having me." I smiled, looking across the audience. "Growing up I had a very all-American, carefree childhood. I had a great family and no major trial or tragedies in my life until…"

The room was silent as I talked about that night on the tracks, and applause rose numerous times when I mentioned the ways God had worked in my life. They weren't applauding me; they were applauding God for all the miraculous things he'd done, for being faithful and never giving up on me.

When I finished speaking, a line of people waited to talk to me. There were men and women, students and adults. After I finished praying with one teen girl, an older man approached.

"I can't believe you're alive. You really should not be alive." His serious tone took me by surprise.

"I know." I'd heard that statement from many people before, and I knew he was right. *God gave me a second chance.*

"No, I'm serious. You really should not be alive. I'm a train engineer. I understand the physics of a train, and I know what it can do. I've seen people get killed. I've been in the engine when people have done exactly what you did, and none of them survived. You said you were run over by thirty-three freight-train cars at fifty-five miles per hour, correct?"

"Yes. That's what the police report says."

"Kristen, you should have been sucked up under that train."

As the man spoke, I thought about the sucking sensation when the train first went over me, and then I remembered the force pressing me down. Butterflies fluttered in my stomach. It had to have been the hand of God, holding me down, protecting me.

"Yeah, you should not be alive, Kristen," the man continued. "I should not be talking to you right now. I'm not a strong believer in God or anything, but there's no other way. God must have been working that night to keep you alive. Your story has strengthened my faith. I'm going to give God another chance."

23

Extraordinary Hope

"Hi, Kristen. I'm a staff member on *The Oprah Winfrey Show.* I heard about your story, and if possible, I'd love for you to give me a call back and tell me a bit more about yourself."

By now I was used to receiving speaking and media requests, but I didn't expect this one, especially while I was still trying to finish school. Didn't God want me to be completely prepared first? I swallowed hard and then wrote down the number and hung up the phone.

Wow. Did I hear that right? The woman's words played over in my mind. *I need wisdom here, God. Is this from you? I'm still in school. Am I ready for this?*

I wasn't shy about sharing my life and my story with people anymore. The thing was, I knew that if I went on *Oprah* and told my story, my life and ministry would become much more public. I wasn't sure I was ready for that. I didn't mind people knowing about my life—I appreciated opportunities to reach out to others through my story—but I was concerned about how difficult it might become for me to finish Bible college as soon as I hoped. Finding a balance between school and ministry was already challenging.

I'd been trying to hold things back until I finished school, but as I prayed about it, I had a deep feeling that I wasn't supposed to be holding the ministry back. I felt that God was reminding me why I was at school and why I started Reaching You Ministries.

This is what it's all about, Kristen: showing people that there is hope. I want you to do this.

The next day I called the staff person from *Oprah,* and she asked me if I would tell her my story. I did and was encouraged by her response.

"Kristen, it's amazing how your life has changed. It's like you're a whole different person," she said. "We'll be in touch."

The next day I heard from a producer. She, too, asked me if I would share my story with her.

"Amazing, Kristen," she said when I finished. "I am interested in having you on the show."

"Really?" I bit my lower lip, unsure I was hearing her correctly.

"Yes, we're planning to do a show on people who've survived suicide and are now using their second chance at life to make a difference in this world. Do you think you'd like to join us?"

"Yeah, I think so."

"Well, let us figure out some things here. You think about it too, and I'll get back to you."

I had several more conversations with her about my appearance on the show. She discussed it with the other producers, and I spent time praying and talking to friends, professors, and my family about the opportunity. A week later the producer and I talked again, and we agreed I would do an interview with Oprah on the show. The next week we taped.

Rain drizzled from the sky as the limo arrived to escort me and my guests from the Moody campus to Harpo Studios. Fifteen minutes later, we pulled into a garage. The driver brought my wheelchair, and I got out. The producer met me and led me to my dressing room. A few minutes later, a woman came in to do my hair and makeup. After she was done, I got dressed.

The monitor on the wall told me that the show was starting. I waited for someone to come and get me when it was time for me to go on stage.

Feeling slightly nervous, I asked God to assure me that this was part of his plan for me. More than anything I wanted a reminder that he was there with me. Less than a minute later, Oprah noticed Bebe Winans in her studio audience. She hadn't been expecting him, but she was excited to see him and asked if he would come on stage and sing. Bashfully, he agreed and walked up to the stage. His smile was wide as he asked Oprah what he should sing.

"Sing whatever you'd like," she told him.

With a contemplative expression on his face, Bebe seemed unsure of what he should sing. Then it looked like he could think of only one song, so he began,

Amazing grace, how sweet the sound,
That saved a wretch like me.
I once was lost, but now am found.
Was blind, but now I see.

My eyes widened. My jaw dropped. I thought back to that night on the tracks.

That's my song... God, I know you're with me. Thank you for the reminder. I know you're here. Thank you for filling this place with your presence. I love you.

As Bebe sang, a sweet peace came over me. Soon the staff was directing me toward the walkway where I would enter the stage.

A video played, and on it was a retelling of the events that led up to my suicide attempt. The video also showed photos of my childhood and teen years. Two men lifted my wheelchair up two steps and into the doorway. Then I heard Oprah's introduction.

"That train came barreling down the tracks, and Kristen laid there, conscious, as thirty freight cars sliced through her body. She should have died that day, but she did not. She says that she is here now with strength and purpose beyond what she ever imagined. Please welcome...Kristen Anderson."

I took a deep breath. *My life and my story belong to you, God. Please use this to save lives and draw people closer to you.*

I rolled down the walkway and onto the stage as the audience applauded. Oprah walked over and shook my hand, smiling warmly. "It's nice to see you."

"Thank you. It's nice to see you too." I returned her smile as I transferred myself onto her couch.

As we did the interview, I felt an overwhelming peace from God. I talked about hope in Christ and the difference a relationship with him can make. These were words I once needed to hear and what I believed other people needed to hear the most. I knew God was with me, and that he was pleased as I spoke from my heart.

Eight minutes later we were done.

I knew things would change after my appearance on *Oprah,* but I couldn't have guessed how much they'd change. At the time, there were a handful of volunteers helping me correspond with people, but after the show aired a week later, hundreds of e-mails started pouring in from people all over the world.

Some were from people who were hurting, who were struggling with depression or suicidal thoughts. Others were from people who wanted to thank me for sharing my story and encourage me in my faith, life, and ministry. They told stories of how God had changed their lives, and many suggested I write my story in a book.

As I read through the e-mails, one in particular stood out. The subject line read: *YOU SAVED MY LIFE.* It was from a young man who wrote that he had been planning to kill himself the day my Oprah interview aired. After his mom left for work, he walked into the living room to turn off the TV. He had a gun in his hand.

As he reached for the remote, he heard me talking about my attempt at suicide and how Jesus had changed my life. He listened as I explained that I want people to know that God loves them, that there's a reason they're here, and that there are things they're supposed to do here.

"I decided then," the young man wrote, "that I wouldn't take my life. It's like you were talking right to me. Thank you."

And as I lay in bed that night, the subject line of the young man's e-mail replayed in my mind. YOU SAVED MY LIFE.

The story I had once been ashamed to tell was now giving people extraordinary hope. Only God could do that. My story helped save another person's life—only because God had first saved mine.

Life, in spite of me.

Epilogue

"Kristen, you need to talk to Tricia Goyer," my friend Margaret told me over lunch one afternoon. I'd first met Margaret at my fund-raiser, and since then we had become good friends. "I met her at a Moody Publishers breakfast in Atlanta and felt God leading me to tell her about you, about your story. She was amazed and said that she would love to talk to you. I think you should write a book with her."

Write a book with her? Wow…people have been asking me to write my story forever. I want to help people, but I'm not sure I want to write a book…at least not yet.

I wasn't exactly comfortable with the idea of sharing all the details of my life in a book or having my life become more public, but deep inside I knew God wanted me to do it. I didn't know when, but I knew I wasn't supposed to it alone.

It's all about you, Lord. Not about me. You gave me this story, this testimony, so I could reach people for you and show them your love, your grace, your faithfulness, and your power. If you are calling me to do this now, with this woman, I will listen. I trust you, God. Please, show me your will.

I met Tricia over the phone. We talked and prayed together, as well as separately, about whether or not we should write this book together. I appreciated Tricia's heart and passion, and over time I felt more and more certain that God was telling me she was the author he wanted to help write my story. Tricia felt the same way, and two weeks later I received an e-mail.

> Hi Kristen,
>
> As I was thinking about this, praying about it the other day, thoughts of the opening came to my mind. Maybe something like this?
>
> Chapter 1
>
> Numb. The cold Illinois wind chilled my body.
>
> Numb. My mind, my heart…

I'm still amazed how God put together that first line, and how the rest of the book came together. There are so many other parts of my story that highlight the goodness and faithfulness of God. I wish I could share them all with you. Although I couldn't include those experiences in these pages, I still hold them close in my heart.

As I finish writing this book, my prosthetic legs are almost done. Ray will finalize them and order cosmetic covers for them soon. For now, I practice walking with them for a few hours at a time around the house. There are moments when I still feel like a toddler; I'm slow and I stumble as I'm trying to balance and walk, but I know my strength will build up over time. My hope is that one day I will be able to use them from the time I get up in the morning until the time I go to bed at night and will need to use my wheelchair only sparingly. I also hope I will be able to walk without crutches most of the time. I'm trusting God with each step.

Reaching You Ministries remains one of my greatest joys. It's an incredible privilege to mentor younger girls, speak to various audiences around the country, reach out to people, and share the hope I've found in Christ. One of my favorite parts is interacting with people one-on-one after I speak, hearing their stories, and assuring them of God's love, comfort, hope, and plans for them too. As people have continued to reach back through the Reaching You Web site, Facebook, and MySpace, the organization has grown. We have built a new Web site, are training more volunteers, and are hiring staff and counselors to help those who are hurting, hopeless, lost, suicidal, and depressed. It's been encouraging to be a small part of it all. I truly love what I do, and I wouldn't trade it for anything in the world.

By the time I hold this finished book in my hand, I will be graduating from Moody Bible Institute with a bachelor of science in biblical studies. Because I want to become a better Bible teacher, I hope to continue my education at a Christian graduate school within the next few years. Someday I would like to do some missions work, do more writing, get married, have children, and earn a doctorate as well. We'll see what God has planned. There are many things I'd like do, but I'm still seeking God's will and timing with all of these things. I want nothing more than to be right next to him, in the center of his will. In all of existence, I've found no better place to be.

Dear reader,

I don't know where you've been, what you've done, or what's been done to you, but I do know this: God knows you, and he loves you just as he loves me. We can both count on his presence, his love, his comfort, his forgiveness, and his guidance, no matter where we go or what we do. I had to learn this lesson the hard way, but I hope that you won't have to.

If you take nothing else away from this book, I hope it has shown you that God is real. If you picked up this book because you are contemplating suicide, I hope my story has shown you that there is always hope. Suicide is never the answer. There is extraordinary hope and life in God's Son, Jesus Christ. Life without measure.

My biggest prayer is that you will begin to have what I have: a personal relationship with him. Nothing compares to doing life with God and his Son. If you don't know him, if you've never made a decision to personally accept his forgiveness and leadership, I encourage you to do so now. The Bible says that no one whose hope is in him will ever be put to shame. You have nothing to lose, only much to be gained. Please don't put down this book until you know that you are right with God, you've been forgiven of your sin, and you will spend eternity in heaven.

God is incredible, and he loves and gives more to us than we could ever ask or imagine. Because of him, I have forgiveness, hope, and joy, in spite of myself. Because of Jesus I have life. I didn't realize what this meant until I almost threw mine away. But now I am thankful for every day...it's a day I get to spend with Jesus and the people he's brought into my life. I feel so blessed.

I pray that you will discover life like this. Abundant life. Eternal life.

Love always, Kristen

Afterword

from Kristen's Mom, Jan Anderson

As hard as everything was after Kristen's suicide attempt, we were so thankful that she was alive. We felt lucky to have another chance at life with her. We knew she should have died—and that God saved her for a reason. It's amazing to see her now. I feel proud and very blessed.

For a year and a half before Kristen's attempt, we tried to get her the help she needed. The doctors told us she suffered from stress and anxiety, but they never used the word depression. We listened to them and followed their instructions, but inside I felt there was something more I needed to do to help my daughter—I just didn't know what. It wasn't until much later that I discovered there was so much more I didn't know. It's hard to believe she kept it all inside.

When Kristen stayed out all night that New Year's Eve, we didn't know where she was. After she came home at 10:00 a.m. the next morning, her dad and I needed her to know that her behavior seriously concerned us. My husband and I needed time to think about the next step. In that moment, grounding her seemed the right thing to do. Kristen wasn't happy with our decision.

The next day, I found a note she'd left for me.

Mom,

I need to go for a walk. I need to clear my head. I'll be back soon.

At first I didn't think anything was wrong. I imagined she did need to clear her head, but several hours later, when she still wasn't home, I got in the car and drove around the town. I looked up and down the streets, and I even checked the park. I saw something yellow and thought it was her jacket, but it was the top of a garbage can.

By this time, I had a feeling that something was wrong.

I went home to see if she had called...and then I heard the sirens. *There must have been a car accident a few blocks away.*

Then the phone rang. It was Kristen's friend from work. She'd heard someone had tried to take their life on the railroad tracks. In my heart I was praying it wasn't my daughter.

Flashing lights lit the neighborhood as I hurried to the park. Policemen and rescue workers raced about. Through the crowd, my eyes met an approaching policeman. "Ma'am, I'm sorry, you can't approach the tracks."

"My daughter is supposed to be home, but she's not and I'm worried."

He asked me what Kristen was wearing, and I told him. He must have known it was her, but he didn't tell me. Instead, he went to talk to his supervisor. By the time he returned, my husband had joined me.

"You should go to the police station for more information," the policeman told us.

The police station was only half a block away. When we got there, a police officer called the hospital. We could tell from his face that it wasn't good news.

He hung up the phone and turned to us. "It was your daughter. She survived, but she lost both legs. Her right leg was severed below the knee, and her left leg was severed above the knee. They're taking her into the operating room right now."

Shock set in. My heart ached. Kristen was in surgery, and I wasn't there. Mothers are supposed to protect their children. She needed me and I wasn't there.

Tormenting thoughts flashed through my mind. *What did I do? What didn't I do? Was I too strict? Was I not strict enough? What did I miss? Why didn't I know? How would she survive without her legs? How will she cope? Will she try again?*

Part of me was in disbelief, wishing I could wake up from this nightmare. It wasn't until I saw Kristen lying in intensive care that everything became real.

Seeing my beautiful seventeen-year-old daughter with no legs was overwhelming. I wanted to trade places with her...take the pain away...give her my legs. I could barely stand to see her in pain and not be able to do anything about it. I didn't want my baby girl to have to go through this. She was so very young.

In the aftermath of what happened, I never imagined something that tragic could turn into something beautiful. For a long time, Kristen wondered why God had saved her. I just wanted her to be happy. I wanted to do anything and everything I could to help her. But I realize now that no matter what I said or did, I couldn't make her happy. She needed to get her joy from God.

Once she started living for Jesus—learning who he is, leaning on him, and understanding that he wanted a personal relationship with her—he transformed her. And now she inspires so many. Our family was also transformed.

Before all of this, we had raised our children as we were raised. We went to church and Sunday school. Our children were baptized as babies and confirmed in ninth grade. We prayed before bed and before meals, but we didn't know there was more. Looking back, I wish we'd had a more Christ-centered home. We didn't know we could have a personal relationship with Jesus. Through it all, everyone in our family came to know God in a new and different way...but Kristen is the one who paid the price. My heart still aches knowing that.

My husband and I are very proud of our daughter. She's strong, happy, and joyful. Nothing brings me more happiness than when she talks about God and what he's teaching her. She has a light that glows from within when she's sharing.

As parents, we can't always be there for our children. My heart breaks every time Kristen tells her story, especially when she says that after she pulled herself off the tracks she cried for me. She was so close—just across the street—and I didn't know she was there.

But God knew, and he was there with her.

What Kristen has learned is a message for all of us. Each of us can lean on God for strength and wisdom every day. He loves us unconditionally. Only Jesus can change our lives, save our lives.

Resources

Suicide Warning Signs:

- appearing depressed or sad most of the time
- having no hope for the future
- feeling hopeless, helpless, worthless, or trapped in a situation, and having excessive guilt or shame
- talking or writing about death or suicide
- withdrawing from family or friends
- acting recklessly or impulsively
- a change in personality, sleeping, or eating habits
- decreased interest in most activities
- dramatic mood changes
- giving away prized possessions
- writing a will
- poor performance at work or in school
- strong anger or rage
- abuse of drugs or alcohol
- self-harm
- self-hate

If you are concerned that someone you know is depressed or suicidal… First, listen to him or her. Give the person every opportunity to open up and share her struggles and feelings with you. Be patient, understanding, sympathetic, and accepting. If she says that she hates life, she can't handle it anymore, she hates herself, she wants to commit suicide, she wants to die, or something similar, believe her words. And if she won't tell you with her words but is telling you with her actions, listen to and believe those. Don't doubt the seriousness of the situation, the person, or what he or she is capable of. Nobody who knew me ever thought that I would try to commit suicide, but I did. And studies show that most of those who have committed suicide indicated to others that they were in deep despair in the weeks or months before their deaths by exhibiting some of these warning signs.

Second, help that person. Urge anyone expressing suicidal thoughts to get professional help from a doctor or counselor—preferably a Christian counselor. If the person is in immediate danger, call 911 right away. Do not leave this person alone until help arrives. Too much is at risk. Suicidal behavior is a cry for help. Anyone who is still alive, even one who is suicidal, truly wants to live. When someone is talking about suicide, expressing feelings of despair, or exhibiting some of the other warning signs, that person is asking for help.

Third, care for the person. It's important for all of us to have support systems and know that somebody cares for us. We all need people who will love us, encourage us, forgive us, and speak godly truth into our lives. Help this person get connected with a church, a small group, or a support group, and be the best friend you are able to be. Don't expect things to change overnight and don't be afraid. Take one day at a time; lean on and look to God for help and guidance. He will bless you and the one you care for.

Acknowledgments

Words cannot express the incredible depth of gratitude I have for each person who has touched my life in unique and amazing ways. God has used many to bless me and shape my life in ways that I could not have dreamed. I wish I could mention them all in this book. I cannot imagine how different my life would be without their love and influence—especially those I've named below. I truly wouldn't be where or who I am today without them.

I will forever be thankful for my immediate family: my mother, Jan Anderson; my father, William Anderson; my sister, Stacey Andersen; and my brother, Ryan Anderson. You have always been there for me, through thick and thin, loving me, caring for me, supporting and encouraging me. Thank you for everything you've given and sacrificed for me. I will always love you.

My extended family has always been a huge blessing to me as well: my Granny, Jane Reseburg; my Pappy, Ray Reseburg; my aunts, Lynne Munro and Robin Seibel; my cousins, Tim DeSombre, Kim DeSombre-Long, Michelle Vickers, Amy Fraser, and Justin Walston; my brother-in law, Ken Andersen; and my nephews, Jacob and Noah Andersen. Thank you so much for visiting, praying, and sending cards and letters. You've always helped me tremendously; I hope I can be as much of a blessing to you.

Good friends can be hard to come by, but I've had some of the best in the world. I know that God placed each one of you in my life for a reason, and I am so thankful you've been there: Niky Brechisen, Kelley Forsythe,

Joy Hobson, Katie Walker, Dave Izenstark, Brian Dempski, Emily Hennings, Chrissy Juliani, Dan Yanca, Ayla Yanca-Davis, Kristen Hann, Heather Lenox, Kati Sommer, and Alan, Vadin, and Christian Kositzke. You have all felt like family, and I'm so grateful that you've allowed me to be a part of your lives. I hope you will always know how special you are and how very much you're loved.

I also want to thank the medical personnel who either helped me the night of my attempt or assisted me in other ways over the last several years: Brock Millsop, Trudy Maatta, Bill Chebny, Dr. Richard Lind, Dr. Amir Heydari, Ruth Ann Beck, Dr. Richard Bolnick, Dr. Jeffrey Ackman, Jim Kaiser, Ray McKinney, Dr. John Mayer, and Dr. Peter Puthenveetil. You all cared for my health in different ways, but together you invested in a life, my life, and it's been changed in so many ways for the better because of you. Thank you for your investment and for sharing all of your talents and giftedness with me. I hope I will make you proud.

I also want to thank my parents' small group, all of my volunteers, and all of my small-group girls. You have gone above and beyond the call of duty, time after time, and I appreciate you all so much. It's been amazing to have your support, and I've loved doing life with you. I hope you know just how much you mean to me. You will always be in my thoughts and prayers, and I pray we will remain friends forever.

Next, I want to thank those who have made a tremendous investment and impact in my life on a spiritual level. Like Jesus, you've modeled godly behavior before me, and you've worked hard to speak truth into my life. To Brad and Valerie Swartz, Robbie, Pastor Jeff Griffin, Pastor Scott Chapman, Dr. JoAnn Nishimoto, Ron Kempka, Dr. Michael Easley, Dr. Bill Torgesen, Dr. John Koessler, and Pastor Dan Petersen, your investment in my life and ministry is eternal, and I know the rewards that God has for you in heaven are tremendous. I pray I can show my great appreciation for you during our time here on earth as well.

And last but not least, I want to thank some of my favorite people, without whom this book wouldn't have been possible. You have each touched my life in a very special way through this process. It's been incredibly amazing to work with you: my coauthor, Tricia Goyer; my agent, Janet Kobobel Grant; my editors Alice Crider and Liz Heaney; and the staff at WaterBrook Multnomah Publishing Group. Thank you so much for your prayerful, heartfelt, and diligent work. I truly couldn't have done this without you! I hope you will always know how much I appreciate you. God is very proud of you too!

Reaching You Ministries

He reached down from heaven and rescued me;
he drew me out of deep waters.
He led me to a place of safety;
he rescued me because he delights in me.
~Psalm 18:16, 19

God really does delight in you. He knows you, He sees your situation, and He's reaching out to rescue you. Take his hand.

We're here to help too. If you can relate to the pain and despair that Kristen faced, please e-mail us. We would love to help you find the hope and joy that God is offering. Our e-mail Support Team understands what you're going through and they're waiting to talk with you.

We'd also love to pray for you. Send us your prayer requests, so our Prayer Support Team can pray for you.

Visit our website: www.reachingyou.org.

- You'll find encouraging stories and articles from Kristen and others God has helped through extreme hardships.
- You'll discover how you can help Kristen and her team bring the hope of Jesus to those who are struggling.
- You'll also see how you can invite Kristen to speak at your event.